DEFINING MOMENTS

DEFINING MOMENTS

Essential queer stories

EDITED BY PAUL IARROBINO

www.ourboldvoices.com

Defining Moments is set in TypeTogether's Karmina and Karmina Sans and My Creative Land's Above the Sky Extras

Cover photo credits: Peter Steiner, Ehimetalor Akhere Unuabona, Paolo Gregotti, Anita Cavalcanti, Philip Myrtorp, Envato (yurakrasil, wirestock, lucigerma, msvyatkovska, LiliiaRudchenko, EwaStudio, FabrikaPhoto, YuriArcursPeopleimages)

Cover design by Arnel Mandilag

ISBN EBOOK 979-8-9901940-1-4
ISBN PAPERBACK 979-8-9901940-0-7
ISBN HARDCOVER 979-8-9901940-2-1

This book is a tribute to our LGBTQ+ ancestors. Their courage and sacrifices have paved the way for the freedoms we enjoy today. Join us as we honor their memories and share our own stories of resilience and pride.

TABLE OF CONTENTS

Acknowledgments

I am incredibly moved by how this collection of stories morphed over time. Contributors rallied behind the vision of this project from the beginning. I quickly learned that since we were representing such diverse experiences across multiple generations, the use of endnotes and author notes were needed. I didn't want to slow down the narratives but adding context was essential.

I am grateful to friends and beta readers Laurie Olson and David Richeh for sharing their astute observations with our writers. As a result, our stories deepened and expanded, letting more of their world open for us, the readers.

Sittrea Friberg reviewed each story carefully and provided encouraging, thoughtful feedback throughout the editing process. I appreciate her kindness extended to all our contributors and supporting me during this long and windy journey.

This book would not have been possible without the support of my husband, Arnel Mandilag. He joined forces with Laurie Olson to conduct a final review and the two of them formed a powerful, virtual team. Armed with a style guide and keen reading, they cleaned up details we missed along the way and helped clarify anything that might be confusing to you, the reader. I am beyond grateful for their tenacity.

Arnel also contributed his technological and design skills with formatting the book, typesetting, and designing the cover.

I appreciate our authors for their willingness to share their stories, at a time when there is so much polarizing discourse. Keep in mind that this book was written during Florida's "Don't Say Gay" bill and the resulting chaos of book bans, anti-trans legislation and revisionist history, all designed to silence us. It is more important than ever for us to tell our stories—our defining moments—the way we experienced it. We must speak our truths. There's too much at stake not to.

Thank you writers for your willingness to be vulnerable and share your narratives. We had multiple forms of feedback along the way and it wasn't all easy. We met virtually for several months to offer peer review and feedback. I am encouraged by our connections and I hope new friendships have emerged from this experience.

I am thankful for funding from the Regional Arts & Culture Council and believing in my original vision. Their financial support helped underwrite the costs attached to such a large undertaking.

And, I thank you for selecting our book. I hope you enjoy it as much as we did creating it.

—Paul Iarrobino

Introduction

When embarking on this journey of assembling writers and creating my own narrative, I was committed to representing as much diversity as possible. In broad terms, I was hoping to represent our rich intersectional identities without restrictions. Through various phases of editing and peer review, all of us dug deeper to reveal our authentic narratives. This process could be intense and time consuming. Sadly, we lost some folks along the way.

When reading these short stories, I encourage you to approach each one as a unique treasure; distinctively written and reflecting each author's voice. Because we have more than fifty years separating our youngest and oldest storyteller, be aware how much our language has evolved over time. Our older authors grew up during decades before pride marches, marriage equality and a growing list of acronyms. The word "queer" was not worn with a badge of honor. We asked each writer to present their experiences authentically and we respect their use of language to reflect their history.

Since there's a variety of time periods represented, we included endnotes and author notes to provide historical context. We hope these stories challenge you to reflect on your own defining moments and to learn more about our personal histories attached to broader societal shifts.

A major motivation for me with creating this new body of work was to record our history as we experienced it. While pulling these stories together, we were acutely aware of the growing political and social polarization in our country. We can never take our human rights for granted. These stories are testament to that. We must continue to speak our truths.

Now, a word about content and trigger warnings. Life itself is a complex range of experiences that define who we are in this world. Childhood trauma, racism, homophobia, transphobia, internalized oppression, reconciling our religious and spiritual beliefs, discovering our first love, coming out, finding our chosen family, is just a starter list. It's impossible to know if any of this material is triggering. I do want you to know, decisions to include these experiences were not taken lightly. In the end, we took this risk to fully show up to our readers.

Most of all, we hope you will reflect on these stories long after you have read them. They are the types of stories worth discussing with others. What stories resonate with you and why? What are your defining moments and why? I hope you enjoy your experience with us and would love to hear from you.

—Paul Iarrobino
www.ourboldvoices.com

The Undefined

By Jamison Green

For the first 14 years of my life, I tried to be the daughter my parents wanted. After all, they had chosen me. I was adopted, not an accident of birth for them. Someone else passed me along, through an adoption agency in Oakland, California, to people who wanted a child. A girl. My adoptive parents had gone through the screening and waited over a year for the call in December 1948, informing them that there were several baby girls available who fit their profile. They were invited to come in and select one. I was 4 weeks old.

In those days, adoption agencies tried to match children to the adoptive parents' ethnicity, religion, and physical attributes. The objective was to reinforce the bonds between the parents and the child and to obscure the temptation of neighbors or strangers to conjecture that the child was "unnatural." A couple that was unable to conceive might be considered defective, so the children should appear as much like the adoptive parents as possible. The new parents should have no doubts that the child could grow to be "naturally" their own. My mother told me I was the first baby they brought out for her and my father to see. And after a few minutes of inspection, they offered to bring forth another available infant. My mother protested, "No, I don't want to see any others. This one is fine." I wonder, did they let her hold me? She recalled that she didn't want to feel as though she'd chosen her daughter like she'd selected the best cabbage at the grocery store.

That made me feel better than a cabbage. I was glad they chose me, but by the time I was 3 years old, I felt they were uncomfortable with me. I knew they loved me, but they were growing increasingly frustrated with my insistence on wearing boys' clothes. I was lucky that they believed children should be free to explore the world and to express themselves. But they also believed that it was a parent's job to teach their children the social rules and the moral values they would need in order to conform and to succeed in life. At times I felt fully myself and comfortable with my parents and with the world. At other times—whenever I would have to put on a dress for any reason—I felt constrained, miserable, and invisible.

About a week after my 4th birthday, the whole family, including my recently adopted baby brother, was on my parents' bed looking through the Sunday newspaper. It came up that Prince Charles of England was having his 4th birthday, too. Recognizing that I was a few days older than the future King and knowing that I was adopted, I realized that Charles and I must have been twins. Because I was a girl, I could not be King of England. They needed their firstborn to be the King, so I had to be sent away to be adopted in America so Charles could inherit the throne. I knew even then that I could never be a queen or a princess. But how did the mother queen know that about me?

In elementary school—in fact, all the way through high school—I had to wear skirts or dresses to school. There was no getting around it. In the second grade, I had seen a particular brand of black high-top tennis shoes on TV that promised to make me run faster and jump higher than any other shoes. I just had to have them, and I begged my parents to buy me a pair. After weeks of resistance, my parents miraculously agreed that the world wouldn't end if I wore these shoes for playing sports. I was ecstatic. My mother took me to the shoe store. In spite of the salesman's clear surprise that a girl would even want such shoes, he found a pair that fit me, and my mother bought them. I couldn't wait to wear them to school.

But my dreams were dashed before the first recess. My teacher gave everyone else a reading assignment to keep them busy. Then she called me up to her desk. She quietly told me I could not wear those shoes.

"WHY?" I bellowed, disturbing the entire class.

"They are not appropriate shoes for a girl," she said softly but sternly, staring straight into my eyes.

"But I NEED them on the playground!" I whispered my lament.

"You must go home now and change your shoes. You can bring them back in a box and put them on after the recess bell rings. But you must have your saddle shoes on and those black things put away in the box before the class bell rings."

"But..."

"No arguments; those are the rules."

I walked home in despair. My mother comforted me and said she was sorry, but we had to conform to the rules. She drove me back to school with my saddle shoes on my feet and my prized high-tops in a shoebox. I never took them back to school again. Once the recess bell rang, and by the time I had them laced up, I barely had time to run across the playground before I had to unlace them and switch to those saddle shoes. I was thwarted at school, but I ran faster and jumped higher all over my neighborhood.

One day when I was in the third grade, I brought a cap my father had given me to school to play with. It was his World War II khaki Army Garrison cap with his sergeant stripes. At recess, I went off to one side of the yard to be alone. I put the cap on and began to exercise my imagination by marching in a small circle and humming to myself. Suddenly, I was pelted by small rocks, then bigger ones. I looked up to see several older boys and girls, and they were shouting at me. "Take off that hat!!" "You can't wear that!" "Girls can't wear that!"

"I can wear it!" I shouted back. I was trapped against the chain-link fence, and they were closing in. "My father gave it to me," I yelled. "It's mine to wear! Stop throwing rocks!! Stop it!" But they just yelled louder and threw harder, eventually attracting the attention of the fourth-grade teacher. She came up behind them and commanded them to stop.

"Now, what's going on here?" she demanded.

"She can't wear that hat," a blond boy with a fresh crew cut asserted indignantly.

"Run along now," the teacher told them, "and no more rock throwing." And to me, she said, "You should have known better than to wear that. Those hats are not for girls. Now go play with your classmates." My assailants laughed at me as they dispersed. I was simultaneously crushed and angry, which made me feel exhausted. I didn't speak to anyone at school for the rest of the day. I took the cap home, put it in my closet, and only put it on when I was alone in my room. The cap still made me proud of my father, but it also made me feel lonely.

By seventh grade, I began to rebel by making my own "school survival uniform." I wore gym shoes with white athletic socks; a plain, pleated skirt; a white. button-down, oxford shirt; and either a dark-colored Pendleton shirt or a baggy cotton jacket. For cold weather, I wore a heavy, gray. wool "car coat" that was as much like a Navy pea coat as I could find. I never had to struggle with what to wear to school because I wouldn't wear anything else. Yes, people made fun of me. My father, who was generally supportive of me, got mad at me now and then, asking, "Why can't you dress nicely like the other girls?" Sometimes at school or on the street, someone would call me queer or a dyke. I had no idea what those words meant, but they sounded derogatory to me. Still, I preferred to endure their teasing rather than wear clothing that made me feel like I was living a lie.

I was not a total outcast, though. I actually had lots of friends. I was good at sports, so people wanted me on their teams. I could tell jokes, I could sing, and I performed at school assemblies. I did get thrown out of Home Economics because I was inept (mostly uninterested) in the class projects. I was disruptive and told stories and engaged in distracting conversations while the "good girls" were trying to follow the assigned recipe or master the art of sewing. My counselor, home ec teacher, and woodshop teacher conferred and agreed to give me a chance to do something different. So, I was sent to the boys' woodshop class. What a relief that was! At first, the boys laughed and teased me. But before long, it was clear that I was just as good at woodworking and mastering the tools as they were. Since there was no boy in the class named Bill, they started calling me that.

It wasn't my right name, but it sure felt better than the very feminine name my parents had given me.

For a long time, I had already been trying on names that fit me better. I went through a series of names over the years: Chip; Packy; Squirt; Thor, God of Thunder. I would announce the name to my family and tell the kids in the neighborhood to just call me that for a while. Nobody fought me over it, but then none of those names ever really stuck. "Bill" was more distinguished than any of my earlier experiments, though it still wasn't quite right. I finally found my name while watching a *Man from U.N.C.L.E.* TV episode. The entire story revolved around a mysterious character named Jamison. The main characters on the show, Napoleon Solo and his faithful sidekick, Ilya Kuryakin, were terrified that Jamison was back. Jamison, apparently, was the most accomplished, intelligent, powerful, and intimidating villain that either of our heroes had ever faced. They thought Jamison was done-in at their last encounter, but no! Jamison was back, and they were afraid. This was early in 1963, and no pronouns ever identified Jamison as a man or a woman, which at the time was an unusual rhetorical convention. Judging by the fear shown by our intrepid protagonists, I reasoned Jamison must have been a man. That was what we were supposed to think, of course. But at the end of the episode, it was revealed that Jamison was a beautiful woman! The story was suspenseful, and the surprise ending was astonishing. Right then, I knew my name. I didn't know if I would grow up to be a woman or a man, but whichever I turned out to be, I wanted to make an impression, just like

Jamison. Not that I wanted to be an evil villain, but I did want to be respected for my intelligence and whatever other admirable qualities I might develop someday. I didn't tell my parents about my new name yet, but I started telling a few friends at school. I started using the name Jamie for short because it seemed cute, safe, and androgynous.

Puberty was a difficult time for me. I could tell I wasn't having the same feelings as most of my peers. I wasn't interested in dating and never thought about intimacy with another person. Masturbation was fine because that was private. I imagined myself as an androgynous young man—not aggressive but not feminine either. I had crushes on several girls who were not friends of mine and a few boys, too. But under no circumstances could I ever express a romantic or sexual interest in another person. No matter who I might choose to express my attraction to, such a declaration would cause people to make assumptions about me that weren't true. If I showed interest in a girl, people would say I was a queer, whatever that was. I still didn't know, but I did understand that other kids called me queer sometimes and made jokes about anyone who was friendly to me. If I showed interest in a boy, people would just think I was a girl, which I knew also wasn't true. Regardless, now I was fully aware that I could never be the daughter my parents wanted. I knew my name, but I still didn't know what I would become.

Going off to college in the fall of 1966 was a high point in my life. My parents made me take some skirts, dresses, nylon stockings, and other feminine accessories. After I settled into my room at the women's dorm, I threw all of those things in the trash bin in the building's basement. I was free! I never told anyone the name my parents had given me. Instead, I always introduced myself as "Jamie; that's short for Jamison." I walked off campus one afternoon and found the Social Security Administration office. I informed them that I was changing my name and asked for a new Social Security Card. Then I took that card to the University Administration building and asked them to change my name on my transcripts, and they did.

I had my first intimate relationship—with a woman—when I was a freshman at the University of Oregon. She was bright and vivacious. She dressed like a British mod girl[1], which was very unusual for Eugene, Oregon, in 1966. And while young men pursued her, she pursued me. We were together for three years, and we remain friends to this day. She's married to a man now, and she identifies as bisexual. But back then, we were both still figuring ourselves out. I had plenty of male friends, and some of them even indicated they were interested in being sexual, but I never felt that would be right for me. I couldn't imagine how they saw me as female. Now, thinking about it over 50 years later, perhaps they were attracted to the masculinity in me and felt that it would be safe for them to explore.

It was early in that first relationship, as I was walking from my dorm to the art building one winter morning, it suddenly dawned on me that I was "cross-gendered." That was the only word I could think of to describe myself. It was as if the "wires" were crossed between my brain and my body. My brain saw the world through the eyes of a young man. My body felt a lot like a young man, even though there were parts of my body that—if other people could see them—would make them think that I was a young woman. But I always knew I was not going to grow up to be a woman. I couldn't imagine myself functioning in society as an adult woman. It was simply impossible. And thus began a search for the path I could follow in negotiating the boundaries between male and female. I wanted to explore all the rules and expectations that those two types of humans were supposed to follow. I wanted to be seen and understood as a human being who didn't fit the system but was a valid human being just the same.

I knew I was part of the queer community, and I tried to fit in as a lesbian for 22 years. But I was not a woman. In spite of some body parts that some trans people might characterize as birth defects, I never thought that my body was wrong. I just pretended I didn't have a body. I wore the clothing I wanted to wear and found jobs where I was allowed to dress in men's slacks and shirts. I worked in construction, I painted apartments, I became a writer and a manager of writers in corporate settings. I was given leeway because I was creative. My imagination and my skills with people, concepts, and language were valued. But I still felt largely invisible—even in the queer community.

In 1978, I told my parents that the woman they knew as my roommate was actually my partner and my lover. I wanted her to be welcomed into my family as more than just a guest. My mother had a small fit and accused my partner of using me and then proclaimed our committed relationship was a phase. But my father looked hard at me while she finished her rant. Then he said, with great deliberation, "I'm sorry...if my attitude...made it so hard for you...to tell me something so important about who you are. Of course, she will always be welcome in our home."

My father died in 1987. He was then the age I am now, 75. I know he was proud of me. And if I have any regrets, a big one is that he did not live to see me through my transition to living in a male body. Even if he might have struggled with my transition, he would have been a source of comfort for my mother.

In 1988 at age 39, after over 20 years of struggle, research, and introspection, I committed myself to a medical transition and to living the remainder of my life as a man. When I told my mother, she slammed her tiny fist on the arm of her chair and declared, "I forbid it!"

I smiled and said, "I'm sorry, Mom. I'm almost 40 years old, and you can't do that. I know you feel like I'm doing this to you, but I'm doing it for me. I've struggled with the difference between my body and my gender my entire life. Now I've learned there's something I can do about it, and I owe it to myself to check it out. It's not an overnight thing, it takes years sometimes. And if at any time along the way it doesn't feel right, I can stop."

"Well...well...well," she sputtered. "Don't tell your brother!"

I laughed. "Yeah, Mom, like he's not going to notice!" So I called my younger brother that evening and told him. His response was, "Well, if that's what you need to do to be happy, you always were like my big brother, anyway."

At that time, there was almost no visible transgender community, no trans movement, and no internet resources to search for anything. Miraculously somehow, I managed to find a few of the pioneers: Steve Dain[2], Lou Sullivan[3], Jason Cromwell[4], and Jude Patton[5], and they welcomed me into their ranks. Lou Sullivan, who died in 1991, was the first publicly known, gay-identified trans man. He bequeathed to me, as a fellow writer, his quarterly *FTM Newsletter*[6] and his mailing list of 232 people scattered across the globe. He also left me his fledgling, San Francisco-based, support group called FTM (for "female-to-male"). In Lou's absence, volunteers rallied, and together we grew that little group. By 1999, when I stepped away from the group to let others lead, it was the world's largest information and networking group for trans masculine people.

Since 1994, I've helped to drive trans and LGBTQI+[7] policymaking and legislative efforts in California and nationally. I worked for years to increase trans peoples' access to medical care and to encourage medical education about LGBTQI+ people. I was elected president of the World Professional Association for Transgender Health[8] in 2011 just months after earning a doctorate in Equalities Law in the United Kingdom. I have participated in revising health and human rights standards from the American Psychiatric Association and the World Health Organization as well as from national, state, and municipal governments around the world. Still, however, the work of belonging, of fitting in, of being safe in society, remains largely unfinished for trans people like me.

My mother died in July 1995. She resisted accepting my transition until her last few months. She and my father had both accepted my name change when I was in college. But when I told her about my plans to transition, my mother reverted to calling me by the feminine name they had given me, as if to freeze me in time. But she was not strong enough to stop me. I persisted in maintaining a relationship with her. It was often painful to have her refuse to look at me. She constantly questioned me, then shut down if I tried to tell her about any of my successes or accomplishments in gender education, laws, or policies. She didn't want to hear of any praise I had received. She wanted everything to remain as it had been before I broke the rules of gender. But in her last few months in the nursing home, she referred to me as her son. I visited her every day. Watching her struggle to breathe, I silently begged my father's spirit to come and get her. She passed in the night shortly after I kissed her forehead and told her I loved her. When she died, my brother and I became orphans.

A few weeks later, at the closing session of the first FTM Conference of the Americas, held in San Francisco in August 1995, I stood on the stage looking out at the expectant faces of the more than 400 people. People who had come from many states and countries to be in the presence of people like themselves—many for the first time in their lives. In many ways, like me, all of them were orphans, too. I had not prepared any remarks, and I was so moved by all these people staring at me, I burst into tears at the podium. In my keynote speech three days earlier, I had described the many challenges people like us faced in society, the ways we found to cope with our shame and isolation, and our obvious need for community. Rhetorically, I had asked, "Who's driving? Are we there yet?" At the beginning of the conference, those questions were food for thought. But now, at the end of the conference—after three days of workshops where bonds were forged and dreams ignited—all I could say through my tears was, "Who's driving?" And more than 400 beautiful people who were hungry for rights, for healthcare, for community, for belonging, shouted back in unison: "We are!" I knew at that moment I was part of something much bigger than me, something very real, and together we would change the world.

Trans people are asking only to be ourselves, to lead healthy lives, and to be safe in our communities. We don't want to erase all genders or the differences between women and men—well, some might say things like that, but there are many ways to see the world. No one can force another person to change or abandon their gender or their sexual orientation. There is no need for LGBTQI+ people to hide or be ashamed of themselves. So, know this: What trans people are asking for is a paradigm shift in the way society values all human beings.

I envision a world without shame or fear of difference. I imagine a world in which gender and sexual orientation are not prisons but instead are safe, free, and diverse dwelling places of the human spirit. I want a world in which people don't have to die because other people are afraid of their differences. I hope for a world where we are all free to be ourselves and where harming others is inconceivable and morally wrong.

This is my life's work, defined for me at birth, though it took me almost half a lifetime to discover it. I am a member of the undefined, the debated ones, the reviled and discarded ones, the ones that many today seek to erase. I will not stop fighting for our collective dignity. I thank my adoptive parents for the foundation they gave to me, a mysterious baby who otherwise might have been just a cabbage.

Endnotes

1 British mod style refers to a style of dress originating in the United Kingdom in the 1960s, typified by (especially for young women) miniskirts, bell-bottom trousers, boots, bright colors and bold patterns, and large, often brightly colored plastic, geometric earrings.

2 Dr. Steve Dain (1939–2007) was the first famous trans man in the United States. He transitioned in 1976 while he was employed as a high school girls' physical education teacher in Emeryville, California. He was fired from his job, and he fought in court to get it back, which resulted in national attention. He was featured in the 1984 film, *What*

Sex am I? He helped many trans men get reliable medical information about how transitioning from female to male would affect their bodies.

3 Louis Graydon Sullivan (1951–1991) came to San Francisco from Milwaukee, Wisconsin, in 1975 with his boyfriend, who encouraged Lou's gay male identity but was unable to accept him when Lou took steps to change his body medically. Lou's diaries, in which he boldly documented his sexual and gender evolution, are now housed in the San Francisco Public Library and have been curated by Ellis Martin and Zach Ozma into an acclaimed volume: *We Both Laughed In Pleasure.*

4 Anthropologist Jason Cromwell (1952–) was an early volunteer at the Ingersoll Gender Center in Seattle, Washington, (founded in 1977) where he helped lead support groups for trans men. His book, *Trans Men and FTMs*, was published in 1999. I collaborated with Jason to create the first FTM Conference in 1995, working with a local team of volunteer organizers in San Francisco. He oversaw the 1990 publication of the third edition of Lou Sullivan's classic pamphlet, Information for the Female-to-Male Crossdresser and Transsexual.

5 Jude Patton (1940–) is a licensed therapist and physician's assistant who transitioned from female to male in 1974 and ran support groups for trans people in southern California. He served on the board of directors for the Harry Benjamin International Gender Dysphoria Association (renamed WPATH in 2007) from 1979–1985. In 1982, he and

three trans women formed the first American Civil Liberties Union (ACLU) Transsexual Rights Committee. He has delivered hundreds of educational lectures and made many television appearances intended to educate the public about trans people. Today, he is a passionate advocate for research and improvements in care for transgender elders.

6 *FTM Newsletter* was a quarterly publication launched by Lou Sullivan in 1987 that began to connect trans men from around the world before the Internet was widely available. A week before he died of AIDS in 1991, Sullivan asked Jamison Green to take over for him and make sure that people who relied on the newsletter as a source of reliable information and community connection would not be cut off from this important resource. Jamison led the FTM International organization from 1991–1999. With help from many volunteers, and a series of editors and contributing writers, the group's members continued the publication. The final issue of the *FTM Newsletter* was published in December 2007 (No. 65). By that time, the Internet was a more efficient method of communication and more widely available. Read all the issues on the Digital Transgender Archive (https://www.digitaltransgenderarchive.net).

7 LGBTQI+. Acronym for Lesbian, Gay, Bisexual, Transgender, Queer/Questioning, Intersex, plus (whatever new terms evolve).

8 World Professional Association for Transgender Health (WPATH) was established in 1979 by a small group of doctors. This educational organization for physicians, psy-

chologists, social workers, nurses, lawyers, and related professionals who research, treat, or counsel transgender people today has roughly 4,000 members worldwide. WPATH produces the *Standards of Care for the Health of Transgender and Gender Diverse People* and also provides training for professionals who are interested in providing that care to be more cognizant of the needs of trans people. For more information, see www.wpath.org.

Jamison (he/him) always knew he would be a writer, a career goal that led to many adventures. He earned his M.F.A. in Creative Writing from the University of Oregon. Since then, he has taught legal writing, skiing, and gender studies. He performed in rock bands, percussion ensembles, and musical theater. He has written for major corporations and led nonprofit organizations. He changed anti-discrimination laws, reformed insurance industry and healthcare delivery practices — all while publishing numerous articles and books on a variety of subjects. His best-known book is Becoming a Visible Man. *Learn more at jamisongreen.com.*

The Undefined

My Life Celebration

By Joshua Thomas

As a Black kid growing up in Galesburg, Illinois, I was treated differently because of my identity. My White friends' parents would not allow them to hang out with me because they perceived me as a threat solely based on the color of my skin. My friends would tell their parents, "Don't worry. Joshua is the whitest Black person you'll ever meet," or "He is a White man trapped in a Black person's body." With time, I internalized these phrases and began using them in order to be accepted by my peers and their parents.

This wasn't the only identity that separated me from my peers. At 7 years old I had a crush on another boy. I felt this attraction but didn't have the language to articulate my feelings. Those feelings weren't reflected in my community. While riding in the car with my dad I asked, "What is it called when you think a boy is cute?" Looking at me in the rearview mirror, he replied, "Only boys can think girls are cute, and only girls can think boys are cute." At that moment I thought there was something fundamentally wrong with me. Overwhelmed with confusion and shame, I decided to keep my feelings a secret. I often prayed to God, "Please, spare me of this sin," and I would cry myself to sleep.

The older I got, the more I grappled with and dissociated from my identities. I hid my true sense of self. I saw myself as someone who wasn't worthy or deserving of happiness and love. From what the world was telling me, I believed I couldn't be trusted; that I posed an imminent threat; that I was inherently inferior to my White peers; and that I was condemned for my sinful sexual attraction. With a disapproving undertone, my mom would occasionally ask me, "Why are you walking like that? Are you gay? If you are, you know you will go to hell."

Her comments undermined my self-confidence, and I felt self-conscious when expressing myself. I was overly concerned about how I walked, talked, and carried myself. I tried to appear more masculine. I avoided forming close connections with other Black and gay people. I didn't want to be perceived as the stereotypical Black person or to reveal my sexual orientation. And I learned to tolerate jokes, slurs, and discrimination towards other Black and gay people. My oldest brother would tell his friends, "Joshua is going to be the gay one." Feeling ashamed, I would stomp and shout, "No, I am not!"

When I was 10 years old, I was sexually abused by an older man who lived in my neighborhood. He took advantage of my curiosity and my lack of self-worth. After I managed to disengage from him, he would occasionally drive by my house to see if I was home. Whenever I saw his car coming down the road, I'd panic and hide. Although I was terrified, I was even more scared to tell my mom. I thought to myself, "Would she disown me? Would she think I deserved it because of my attraction to men? Would other family members find out and further humiliate me?"

In 2012, during my sophomore year in college, I accidentally came out as gay. It happened while I attempted to mediate a family feud on Facebook between my dad and my sister. She exclaimed, "Joshua, it's so funny how you try to act like the family mediator, but you are the one who keeps secrets from the family." I countered, "Are you referring to me being gay? There you go. Are you happy now?" In tears, surrounded by my peers in the college cafeteria, I quickly called my dad. As soon as he answered, I cried out, "Dad, I'm gay! Gabby hinted at it on Facebook, forcing me to come out." Infuriated, he said, "She did what? Why would she do that? Can I call you back? I'm pissed off! I can't believe she did that to you!" Immediately, he hung up the phone to speak with my sister. A couple days later, while talking to my stepmom, she told me, "Your dad is upset you didn't feel comfortable telling him. He thought you two were close and that you could tell him anything." At that moment, I felt my dad's unconditional love and acceptance for me.

Now that the secret was out, I started dating men. But I still struggled with a lack of self-worth, and I still tolerated negative behavior. I found myself in an unhealthy relationship with a younger, White man for nearly three years. We instantly connected when we first met. With time, we devolved into periodic verbal abuse, physical outbursts, and instances of unfaithfulness. It was hot and cold. When things were good, they were great. When things were bad, they were toxic. We would fight, break-up, and then get back together after a few weeks. Our relationship was like a drug to me. I would do anything for him. He was my first love. I thought I could be my true self with him. Although I knew he loved me, re-enactments of our past traumatic incidents prevented us from having a consistently healthy relationship.

Weeks later, we were on spring break together in Panama City, Florida. It was March 13, 2014; a date I will always remember. We had just shared a day of singing, dancing, and enjoying the beach together with our friends. I chose this time to tell my boyfriend, "I love you, and I can imagine spending the rest of my life with you." To my surprise, he sarcastically said, "My ex used to tell me that all the time." Heartbroken, I threw down the backpack that I was carrying for him and stormed off. Barefooted, with no cell phone or shirt, I got lost looking for our motel. At this point, it was dark, and I was in a panic. Seeing me crying, people would stop to ask if I needed assistance, but no one could help me locate our motel. When I finally found the motel, our friends were there, but my boyfriend wasn't. They said they hadn't seen or heard from him and figured he was lost as well. Quickly, I rinsed myself off to calm down and went out looking for him. Before I could make it out the door, he arrived. He was enraged and yelled at me to leave. Emotionally drained, I pleaded with him to try to work it out. But he kept yelling at me to leave. I shouted at him, "You're talking to me as if I mean nothing to you. If I ran off, and even got hit by a car, you wouldn't care." He shouted back, "Do it. I don't care!" I flung the door open and sprinted towards the road. At that moment, I intended to end my life. Nothing in my mind told me to stop. It was like the starting gun going off in a race, and my mind went completely blank.

The next day, I woke up in the hospital, and a nurse immediately told me, "Last night, you were hit by a car. You broke your tibia and fibula. You experienced a compound fracture (one of your bones pierced through your leg). You also have a severe concussion. You've had two surgeries, one last night and one this morning. During the last surgery, they put a metal rod in your leg so you can be weight bearing while your bones heal." Lost for words, I responded, "Can I have a glass of water?" Soon after that, I went unconscious again. When I woke up, my boyfriend was at my bedside, crying and profusely apologizing. I felt weak from the loss of blood, and I was in excruciating pain. I didn't have the will to tell him to leave. I was afraid that it would turn into another outburst between us. So, he stayed in the hospital with me for a couple days. After he left for Illinois, I was alone. I told my parents not to come yet because I wanted to sleep and regain my strength.

Alone in the hospital I felt I had lost it all—my Division 1 track career, my schooling, and potentially, my leg. I thought to myself, *This is a make-or-break moment for me depending on my perspective. I can either create meaning out of this situation or I can let it further break me down.* While battling a severe infection, I took six weeks off from school to rest, recover, and visualize my life after graduation. During a conversation with my parents, they told me they heard that I was in a toxic relationship and that it was the cause of my suicide attempt. My parents said, "We can't tell you what to do, but please ask yourself if this is the type of relationship you want to be in. You almost lost your life." I was still afraid I would go back to my boyfriend as I had done in the past. But they were right. At that moment, I summoned the courage to end the relationship with my boyfriend. I told myself, "I need to get away as far as I can from him." Instantly, I thought about my aunt in Portland, Oregon. I called her, told her what happened, and asked if I could live with her until I got settled. "Of course, but you shouldn't come if you're running away. You'll end up going back," she cautioned me. I told myself, "I will always love him. It's not that I can't have him, but we're not good for each other."

At 22 years old, four months after my suicide attempt, I summoned my courage and moved to Portland thinking my circumstances would change. However, with Portland being predominantly White, I went weeks without seeing another Black person and frequently experienced anti-Blackness and homophobia. On one occasion, while riding the bus, a White person refused to sit next to me. It was a completely open seat, but they waited until a seat opened up next to another White person. When I shared this experience with my White boyfriend at the time, he said, "I doubt that's the case. I think you're perceiving the situation wrong." Another day, while waiting to take the train, a White man, for no apparent reason, started calling me a n***** and faggot. My heart was racing, and I started sweating. I tried walking to the other side of the track, but he followed me. To dodge him, I hurried onto the train when it arrived. When he also boarded, I quickly jumped off and ran to the next car. Although I was relieved that I got away, I knew that racism and homophobia is never really over.

With time, these experiences impacted my mental health, leaving me believing I was inferior, invisible, and voiceless. I eventually wished that I had died in my suicide attempt. I had moved from my home state of Illinois with the hopes of a better life, but my circumstances followed me to Oregon. Suddenly it dawned on me that something in my life needed to fundamentally change. I asked myself, "What do I need to do to overcome these fearful feelings? I'm tired of feeling this way."

The first thing that came to mind was to go on a spiritual journey. "What the heck does that mean?" I thought. Growing up in a Christian and Seventh-Day Adventist family, religion was one of the root causes of my suffering. I couldn't fathom turning to religion for help, but I listened to my inner voice and sought out spiritual philosophy. Fortunately, within months a coworker introduced me to the Soka Gak-kai International (SGI), a lay Buddhist organization. In the Fall of 2016, eager to learn about the practice, I attended my first meeting. Approaching the door, I asked myself, "How are they going to perceive me as a gay, Black man?" To my surprise, the people hosting the meeting were an interracial (Black and White) lesbian couple. Instantly, all of my doubts and worries vanished.

The SGI Buddhist community assured me, "Everyone without exception possesses the Buddha nature—unlimited wisdom, courage, and compassion. All can obtain happi-ness in this lifetime, regardless of their race, gender, sexual orientation, etc. Through chanting *Nam-myoho-renge-kyo*[1], you can polish the mirror of your life and start to see your authentic self more clearly." Inspired by the encouragement and guidance from this community, on May 7, 2017, I decid-ed to officially become a Nichiren Buddhist. I received the *Gohonzon*[2], a mandala that serves as a mirror reflecting our internal life.

After enshrining my *Gohonzon*, I made a vow to work for my happiness and the happiness of others. I would do this by undergoing my inner transformation. I would challenge myself and find value in all of the hardships that caused me to attempt to end my life. I shifted my perspec-tive to view my circumstances (misfortunes) as opportuni-ties (medicine). I worked to connect and encourage others to live true to themselves and to respect the dignity and sanctity of life. So, I challenged my own disassociation from my identities, my internalized anti-Blackness, and my homophobia. Through chanting, I acknowledged that I isolated myself from the Black and LGBTQ2S+ community because I did not want to be perceived as the stereotypical Black or gay person. I further realized how entrenched I was in the anti-Black and anti-gay sentiments that I had learned from society. I saw how this influenced my view of myself and my interpersonal relationships. With this awareness, I continued my chanting. I challenged these thoughts and beliefs until I experienced a breakthrough.

I instilled within my heart the Buddhist principle: Cherry, Plum, Peach, and Damson[3], as stated by my Buddhist mentor, Daisaku Ikeda[4]. "Just as cherry, plum, peach, and damson blossoms all possess their own unique qualities, each person is unique. We cannot become someone else. A cherry blossom can never become a peach blossom. Nor is there any need for it to try to do so. It would be perfectly miserable if it did. The important thing is that we live true to ourselves and cause the great flower of our lives to bloom." Through this principle, I realized I had tried to become someone else rather than being true to myself and letting my authenticity shine.

With a new sense of determination, in 2018 at the age of 27, I attended my first Pride festival. With a genuine sense of self-acceptance and freedom, I joyfully cheered and danced throughout the march. I reclaimed and embraced my queer identity and its expression. I connected with people who share my experiences and my identity. Later that month while talking to my mom, I asked, "If I were to get married, would you attend my wedding?" Appalled by my question, she replied, "Of course I would attend your wedding. You're my son. God made you who you are, and He makes no mistakes."

"March 13th will be a day you will never forget," I still recall a nurse telling me while I recovered from my suicide attempt in the hospital. Although I didn't quite understand what she meant at that moment, I later realized she was right. Each year on the anniversary of my suicide attempt, I would dissociate from my body. The reminder of the day was too much to bear. I'd suddenly be overwhelmed with shame and survivor's remorse. I was sorry for what I put my body through. I regretted the fear I caused my family, friends, and my broader community. I'd think about a high school acquaintance who lost her father and her only child in a car accident that she and her husband had survived. It pained me to see her and her family grieve over their loss while I remained alive with my shame. I'd often ponder, "Why did these two innocent people lose their lives, but I survived after attempting to take my own life?"

With the fifth anniversary of my suicide attempt approaching, I chanted about my heavy thoughts and feelings. It was the first time I felt I had the tools to acknowledge and affirm those feelings. The vibration from chanting calmed my nervous system while I processed my thoughts. As I chanted, I realized how precious life is. How precious others' lives are. How precious all living things are. And finally, how precious my own life is. Instantly, I began to cry, and I was filled with a sense of gratitude to be alive. I then reflected on all of the things I had accomplished since I tried to end my life: I graduated from college on time, I moved to a new city, I found a full-time job within my degree, I fostered community, and began my healing journey. Embracing myself, I smiled and patted myself on the back for persevering through one of the most challenging periods of my life. I mentally expressed appreciation for chanting *Nam-myoho-renge-kyo* and for my Buddhist principles. I gave thanks for the people, the communities, the moments in nature that held and supported me along the way. The more I chanted, the more my perspective shifted from shame to gratitude. I promised myself that I would live my best life on behalf of the people who lost their lives so suddenly. I promised to continue to heal and to create value out of my past, present, and future experiences.

I've now come to regard March 13th as my Annual Day of Life Celebration. Every year I dedicate the day to honor and celebrate my life. I go soak at Breitenbush Hot Springs and reflect on my accomplishments and my personal growth over the past year. I reaffirm my commitment to my own happiness and to the happiness of others beginning with my friends, family, and the people in my immediate environment.

I noticed how generational trauma has adversely affected my family's interpersonal relationships. Years ago I vowed to model forgiveness and vulnerability with my mom. This led me to chant for happiness for us both and for our mutual forgiveness and respect. While praying, I opened up my heart to forgive her for the things she said and did that hurt me. I forgave myself for the words I said to her and the actions I took that hurt her. Waves of tears poured down my face as I felt a release within my body. A few months later while on the phone with my mom, I shared, "I often catch myself dancing, singing, and acting goofy around the house. I realized that I learned that from you. Thank you for instilling that within me." In another conversation I shared the comments that she made that had hurt me. She apologized, "I was doing the best I knew how then. I recognize some of those things hurt you, and I am learning to do better." During that same conversation, I shared that I was sexually abused, and I shared my fears of telling her as a child. She listened wholeheartedly, affirmed my feelings, and empathized with me. This signified a breakthrough in transforming generational trauma through healing my relationship with my mom.

While chanting to accept my racial identity, I manifested an opportunity to attend a pro-Black training. In the training, the instructor shared the ways in which enslaved Africans hid their culture and how our African vivaciousness is coded within our DNA. At that moment, I felt a wave of gratitude for the privilege of carrying the melanin of my ancestors. I joyfully reclaimed my identity as a person of African descent. Furthermore, through joining a queer-inclusive basketball league, I formed close connections with other Black queers and began participating in occasional gatherings. Following the initial happy hour, I recognized that it was the first time that I gathered with other Black queers. It filled my heart with joy being in the company of people who could fully relate to the complexities of our intersecting identities.

Chanting also helped me become aware of my tendency to engage in sexual activities when I didn't really feel inclined to do so. I thought about my instances of infidelity within my relationships. This recognition prompted me to seek the guidance of a sex therapist in order to explore and understand my sexual encounters more deeply. It became evident that my tendency to have sex without genuine consent was linked to my past experiences of sexual abuse. As an antidote, I started saying "no" when I wasn't interested, and I set firm boundaries for myself. Unpacking infidelity, I made the connection that since I had been cheated on multiple times, I believed that people were incapable of being monogamous. I felt people were not capable of communicating their needs, wants, and desires. If they weren't going to hold themselves to higher standards, then why should I? So when I suspected partners were being unfaithful, I resorted to infidelity as a trauma response. I challenged this notion and my other past behaviors while chanting. I continued working with my therapist to define my own needs, wants, desires, and boundaries. This process has enabled me to communicate effectively with others and to foster self-integrity and mutual respect.

One morning while chanting and engaging in my forgiveness practice, I started forgiving former partners. I internally expressed gratitude for the valuable lessons my relationships taught me. I examined the qualities I want and don't want in a relationship. I personally focused on those areas so I can reflect those same qualities. Regarding the relationship connected to my suicide attempt, I expressed it to myself in this way: "I hope he knows I'm good. I've healed, I'm happy, I'm thriving, and I forgive him and myself." After my chanting session, I checked my phone and saw a Facebook request from him. Hesitantly, I accepted the request. In previous years, any attempts to reconnect resulted in emotional outbursts and in me blocking him. The following day, he messaged me. We expressed mutual forgiveness and acknowledged our individual growth. Despite all of the pain we both endured together, nine years later we could be cordial and maintain good relations with each other.

I'll be honoring and celebrating my 10th Anniversary of Life on March 13, 2024. In my years of reflection, I realized my suicide attempt was a benefit. It has become a defining moment for me. All of these experiences deepened my sense of humanity and my connection to life itself. I have a deeper understanding of suffering, and I empathize with others. I affirm their experiences while also making space to do the same for myself. I feel the gift of self-forgiveness and the gift of forgiveness of others as one of the most powerful forms of healing. And I have learned the importance of having a strong sense of self. By treasuring ourselves, we can bring forth our fullest potential and nourish the potential of others.

Endnotes

1 In 13th-century Japan, Nichiren, a Buddhist reformer, established the practice of chanting *Nam-myoho-renge-kyo* as the means for all people to bring forth their inherent Buddha nature, a life state characterized by limitless reserves of courage, wisdom, and compassion. Nichiren regarded *Myoho-renge-kyo*, the title of the Lotus Sutra, as its essence and added Nam to indicate devotion to its principles. When SGI Nichiren Buddhists chant *Nam-Myoho-renge-kyo,* they infuse their lives with the Mystic Law—the ultimate truth or law of life. Through this practice, practitioners demonstrate the wisdom to navigate effectively through any situation, ultimately creating the most valuable and positive outcomes.

2 SGI Nichiren Buddhist chant to the *Gohonzon,* a mandala inscribed by Nichiren that embodies the Law of *Nam-myoho-renge-kyo. Gohonzon* is an object of respect or devotion and serves as a spiritual mirror to perceive the true nature of our lives and to bring forth the Buddha nature—limitless reserves of courage, wisdom and compassion.

3 Cherry, Plum, Peach, and Damson represent a Buddhist principle that serves as a metaphor, symbolizing that one should refrain from comparing oneself to others. Instead, it encourages individuals to allow themselves to grow and be true to who they are.

4 Daisaku Ikeda (1928–2023) was the third president of the Soka Gakkai and founding president of the Soka Ga-

kkai International (SGI). He is one of the three eternal mentors of SGI Nichiren Buddhism.

Joshua (he/him) is a storyteller, social justice advocate, and community leader in Portland, Oregon. He was born and raised in Galesburg, Illinois, and has lived in Portland for the past 9 years. Committed to liberation, peace, and justice, he's currently employed at Oregon Food Bank as their Equity and Work Culture Manager. He also serves as a Youth Buddhist leader for the Soka Gakkai International, a lay Buddhist Organization. He is a recurring storyteller with Our Bold Voices. As a gay Black man, he has found healing and has found his voice through telling stories. In his free time, he enjoys reading, hiking, biking, and soaking in hot springs.

My Life Celebration

My Summer Love

By John Lucia

The heat. It was brutal. The sidewalk shimmered. Dirt swirling in the air from the nearby subway construction project only added to the misery. I never wore an undershirt that summer. It would add one more layer of dirt and sweat, suffocating me.

Foster's Fine Foods[1] sat on the busy corner of First and Mission Streets in San Francisco. That was a joke of a name considering the questionable fare they served. The bus terminal, across the street from the diner's entrance, gave easy access to travelers and troublemakers.

I needed money for college, so I applied for a summer job at Foster's after high school graduation. The job opening was for a "porter." That was the guy who got all the fun tasks—cleaning the filthy bathrooms, mopping the always greasy floor, busing the grimy tables. I was desperate, so I took the job.

My boss, affectionately named "The Grump" by his employees, was a cigar-chomping, growling bear of a man with a foul temper. My friends were off to swim parties in Marin or camping at the Russian River. I was moping and pouting about having to work because I had no other choice.

It was 1967, and I was 18. I had been a good Catholic high school boy. In my last year before graduation, I had a girlfriend. However, I was struggling with my attraction to men. It was a secret I hid from everyone. But I lived in constant fear that my secret would be exposed, and I felt guilty for having these feelings.

During my second week at work, on a Monday morning, a man walked through the diner doors. The heat outside crackled as the doors closed behind him, forming a weird golden light around him. He looked more like a glowing angel than a mortal man. He wore an expensive silk suit, a perfectly tied tie, and immaculate Italian shoes that clicked as he walked on the terrazzo floors. His crisp white shirt had French cuff links, and his brown hair was perfectly groomed. The image was completed by his ramrod posture and his beautiful hazel eyes. He had an air of dignity and pride about him.

I avoided eye contact with him. I knew it would be dangerous for me to admit that I was attracted to this handsome man. I was afraid that my attraction to men would be discovered. What would my coworkers think of me? And he was probably 10 years older than me.

I kept sweeping the floor and busing tables while I secretly watched him. Now he was in line to place his order. Now walking toward the napkins. Now searching for a table. In his slow-motion wake, he left a trail of gawking cafeteria workers and customers, both men and women. Mouths hanging open, eyes fixed on him as though he were a movie star. I wondered if he knew the effect he had on others.

Soon his daily arrival at the diner became the most important event of my day. What would he wear? Would he look in my direction? Did he even know that I was there? I had my doubts.

One morning, looking directly at me, he asked me my name. I didn't think he would remember it, so I mumbled quietly, "John," and kept working, turning my back to him.

Then, he told me his name: William. It was the perfect name for the perfect man. William. He asked me for the newspaper on the table I was clearing. As I handed it to him, he looked into my eyes. Watching him when he wasn't looking, I always felt safe. Now, as his eyes never left mine, I was terrified. I wanted to stay in the background and admire him from a distance.

Maybe he wasn't gay? I'd seen him speaking flirtatiously with the women in the food line. I watched as he reduced them to giggling and blushing schoolgirls. The men were taken with him, too. Even my boss, The Grump, lit up like a Christmas tree when William was around. Weeks later, I heard him tell William that he was his favorite customer. Really? I had never heard those words out of The Grump's mouth before about anyone.

A few mornings later, William breezed through the door, his elegant sunglasses reflecting the brutal sun. His gaze landed right on me. I pretended not to see him. As he lowered his glasses, he fixed his beautiful eyes on mine, and in a clear and melodic tone he said, "Good morning, John." I was frozen to the spot, too terrified to look up or respond. Somehow, I managed a morning greeting back in his direction.

Instead of getting into the order line, he pivoted and walked toward me. I thought, "Oh dear God. What are my coworkers going to think if they see us talking to each other? Can I crawl under this table?" In a voice just above a whisper he said, "You look like you're working very hard." What was going on here?

"Well, thanks," I managed to answer. He was almost smiling. I frantically wiped the table in front of me. I was sweating like a pig. Later, as I mopped the floor, he looked at me again, this time breaking into a real smile. I half-smiled back and kept mopping, slopping water all over my shoes. He got up to leave, stepped into my line of sight, and said, "Have a great day, okay?" I muttered, "Thanks, you too," and continued mopping feverishly.

He turned on his heel, breezed out the door in his perfect Italian shoes; those fancy sunglasses again planted over his eyes.

I was shaken out of my stupor by The Grump, who said "Nice guy, huh?" As I mopped over his foot, I suspected he knew how mesmerized I was by this man. And he was right—I was. We both watched William disappear into the blistering heat.

I worked the next Saturday, a rarity for me. I assumed it would be another boring day, full of busing and cleaning. I came out of the bathrooms and, not looking where I was going, I ran right into William.

Ignoring my shocked look, he began in rapid fire, "I wondered if you would be here today. I came into the office to do some work. Do you get a break from this drudgery? Want to have a cup of coffee with me?"

At first, all I could do was stand there and stutter. Did he really want to sit down with me—here in the diner—for a cup of coffee? When I recovered, I blurted out, "Yeah, sure," feeling like the 18-year-old simpleton that I was. My heart was beating a mile a minute, realizing that I was going to have coffee here with this handsome man. What would we talk about? I excused myself, went back to the bathroom, and washed my face, trying to get the sweat off me. Oh God.

He was already seated with his coffee when I sat down across from him. Conveniently, he had picked the farthest table from the serving line. I immediately detected the subtle scent he always wore. It was a combination of sweet and musky. Then, timidly, I glanced up and looked into his eyes.

He began with, "So, how long have you worked here?" Then he asked me more about myself. I told him about my Italian family and about school and my graduation. I was surprised how soon I felt at ease with him.

He paid close attention as he listened to my answers. I was surprised by his next question and startled by the intensity of his look as he asked, "And, do you have a girlfriend?" I blurted out, "We're sort of on again off again. I'm not sure it's going anywhere." I waited for his reaction. But Mr. Cool gave me a Cheshire cat smile and took a sip of his coffee. Dead silence.

We continued to talk until he said that he had to get back to the office. As we stood up he said, "I'm going to the movies tonight. Want to go?" My sweaty feet felt like they were rooted to the floor in buckets of cement. Without thinking about what his invitation really meant, I said, "Sure," and I agreed to meet him downtown later. Then, he was gone.

I felt uneasy as I rode the hot streetcar home after work. What were his intentions? He knew I was 18 and that I still lived at home. He told me about his apartment in the Haight[2]. Was he making a pass at me? If so, what was I going to do about it? I was very attracted to him, but I felt he was way out of my league. He was polished, confident, and worldly. I was a porter at a diner.

I borrowed my mother's car to get to the theater. He was waiting outside, dressed in yet another impeccable outfit. "Well, you certainly look cool and rested after a day at work," he said. I was awestruck again by how gorgeous he was. I grinned at him and said, "I feel great. I'm glad we're here." As we walked into the theater, I felt a new sense of pride for being in his presence. At that moment, I felt both grown up and yet very young.

I don't remember the name of the movie. Whatever it was, it came in a distant second to the thrill of being with William. Before the lights went out, his familiar scent wafted into my nostrils. As his lips touched my ear, he said, "I'm getting something to drink. Would you like something?"

Electric bolts zapped up and down my torso. I turned and looked right into his hazel eyes and blurted out, "Coffee." And he was gone. When he returned, he had drinks and a bag of popcorn. Every time he reached for popcorn from the box I was holding, he smiled at me. He leaned up against me, and I could feel his warm body next to mine. It was hard to concentrate on the movie. He was definitely flirting with me.

When the movie was over, he surprised me with, "Would you like a nightcap at my place?" Ah, there it was. He was making his move. He laughed and said, "You should see the look on your face. I promise, I'll take good care of you."

What...what?! I was in full-blown panic mode. While he was giving me driving directions to his apartment, I was wondering if this was a good idea. What if I had to get undressed in front of him? In front of William. What would I do? Was it too late to make excuses? He kept smiling at me, and said, "Did you understand all that? Apartment F. You'll remember?" I nodded my head, my mind in a fog. He smiled sweetly, and we departed for our cars.

I walked up to his apartment building and rang his bell. When he buzzed the door open, I thought, "Well, this is it, kid. You're about to cross over into a new world." What would I do or say? I couldn't possibly make the first move. What if I had been wrong about him? Maybe he was just a nice guy being friendly to a teenager.

When he opened the door, I thought, "How could this charming, sophisticated man be interested in me?" Before I had a chance to start down that rabbit hole, he grabbed me in a tight clench. He pulled me into his apartment hall, slammed the door closed, and kissed me. It was a long, erotic kiss. I heard myself sigh.

The rest of that night was a blur. He slowly undressed me, murmuring his admiration as he explored my body. I was shocked. Was I attractive to him? I hesitated to touch him. He said, "Go ahead," and I nervously unbuttoned his shirt. Soon we were both naked. He had a great body. This was a new experience because I had never been with a man. I kept staring at his beautiful face and couldn't look away.

He was sure of himself, and he was a passionate lover. I was lost in exploring his body, and I loved how he reacted to my touch. I never imagined that my touch could elicit such a reaction from him. It was a revelation. I was lost in the timelessness of our lovemaking and the warmth of his company. We lay in bed afterward, talking, laughing, smoking. I felt at ease with him. He was funny and sweet. He was so much more natural than his usual daytime image portrayed. And I felt less self-conscious around him now.

Our pillow talk turned to William's own story. He was raised on a farm in Iowa. His father wanted him to stay and run the farm, but William had other ideas. He escaped to college, studying business. He took modern dance and drama classes. He wore turtlenecks and dance tights and pretended he was a beatnik. Or as much of a beatnik as Iowans might tolerate.

After college, he went to work for a large computer company in Manhattan and met his first male lover. William commuted into the city from their small upstate New York suburb.

Their relationship broke up a few years later, and William hatched a plan to move to San Francisco—a place he had always thought of as exotic and full of history. He drove across the country in his little MG convertible to start a new job in San Francisco.

We continued to see each other for several weeks after our first date. I was completely smitten with him. He had a surprising grasp of the local cultural and art scenes. He took me to art galleries, the opera, the ballet. We took several trips to the North Beach district to listen to unknown jazz singers in smokey alley bars. We drank espresso coffee at Caffe Trieste, a favorite chaotic hangout for local authors and tourists alike. We would sometimes rummage through

City Lights Bookstore, a disorganized jumble of dusty piles of books stacked everywhere, run by sweet hippie poets. A night at a Moroccan restaurant introduced me to eating with my hands while sitting on the floor. A trip to a new French restaurant out near the ocean exposed me to escargot. I never knew these exciting adventures existed in my own hometown. I was learning about the more worldly part of this wonderful city.

I felt an intimacy and glow whenever I was with him. For this 18-year-old, his attention gave me a satisfaction I had never experienced. He was smart, funny, and handsome. He relished the role of being my teacher and guide, and I enjoyed being his student.

I was learning about myself. I liked William, but I sensed he was "dating around." He made comments about guys he had met, supplying few details of those meetings. I suspected that he enjoyed his status as a single guy in a new city. I realized I was not going to be his exclusive boyfriend. Though this made me sad and jealous, I didn't feel I had an emotional hold on him.

Over dinner one night, he initiated a talk about dating other guys. He asked me how I would feel if he went out with other people. I was hurt, but I knew that my relationship with William would never be what I had hoped for.

After all, I was not quite 19, and I had a lot of life ahead of me. And he was the attractive new guy in town. "You don't hate me, then?" he asked. I laughed, took his hand and said, "I really want us to be friends. That's very important to me." He said, "I really like that. I agree." We both laughed and continued with our meal. It surprised me that I didn't act with more jealousy because he meant so much to me. But I was being honest with myself. I was learning to be more mature and realistic.

Our relationship gradually morphed into friendship. We became "telephone buddies," as we called it. We spoke on the phone almost every night, often blabbing for two or three hours. We continued touring city spots together on weekends. Eventually, as though by unspoken agreement, our sexual relationship stopped.

My summer job at Foster's diner came to an end, and I started community college that fall. I took a part-time job as a florist in an upscale flower shop. Both William and I went through a series of boyfriends—some serious, some not. I introduced him to Peter, a great guy, and they began a relationship that lasted about a year. Eventually, William broke it off.

I felt bad for both William and Peter. How could they ditch their great connection? But William had taught me to bend with the flow of life. He told me that he didn't think he could stay in a long-term relationship with anyone. This really surprised me. He seemed like a romantic person to me. But each time he had been in a relationship with someone, he seemed to lose interest. I eventually came to admire his courage for being so realistic about who he was. That was an important lesson—to be honest about who I am. I learned from him to admit when a relationship was over.

I eventually landed a corporate job that offered me room for advancement and a chance to learn new skills. William was there for me, encouraging me with each upward step I made; always supporting my decisions and reminding me that I could do good work.

In the meantime, men came in and out of both our lives. I met someone, we fell in love, and moved in together. With this new relationship, my connection with William began to change, and I could feel him withdrawing from our friendship. I saw that our student/mentor relationship was fading. I was no longer his student, and he seemed to thrive in relationships where he could mentor young men. Our phone calls slacked off to only one short call a week. In the years that followed, we kept in touch sporadically, but much of our communication was superficial.

A planned move from San Francisco to Portland, Oregon, with my partner brought up many feelings for me. I struggled with guilt about leaving William and my family behind, even seeking counseling to help me sort through my feelings. When I told William about the move, he took the news stoically. Though he feigned interest in my decision, I knew that we were growing even further apart.

I decided the move was best for me. William had taught me to weigh my options when making big decisions and to consider the benefits to me.

In 1994, as I was preparing for the move to Portland, William was diagnosed with HIV[3]. I was stunned and I felt helpless. There was nothing I could do for him but listen to him and be his friend. I didn't want to think about how this would end.

As the months went by, he became quiet and sullen. He began pulling further away from me. We rarely spoke anymore. I knew he wanted to protect his own emotions and the emotions of those of us who loved him. I was losing William to a fatal illness, and I missed the connection we had both outgrown.

After my move, I really wanted to visit William in San Francisco. Our mutual friend, Milton, who called me with periodic updates, told me not to come. He said that William had lapsed into dementia and was now blind and angry and wouldn't know who I was. I cried thinking about how alone William must have felt and how I should have been there to help him through it.

It was as if William were already gone. I felt I never had the chance to say goodbye to the man who helped me become an adult. William died two years later.

I will forever carry William in my heart. He was my first love, someone who paid attention to me, a shy teenager just heading into adulthood. He was also my teacher and my friend, exposing me to culture and joy and new experiences. I learned to develop confidence, to think better of myself, and to trust my instincts because of him. I miss his friendship and guidance.

Endnotes

1 Fosters Fine Foods was a chain of restaurants with numerous locations throughout downtown San Francisco characterized with bold, stylized, red-neon signage. By the early 1970s, all had disappeared from the local landscape.

2 The Haight district, also known as the Haight-Ashbury, drew the attention of youth from all over America. This neighborhood offered a concentrated spot for hippies to gather and experiment with counterculture ideals, drugs, and music.

3 Human Immunodeficiency Virus (HIV) is the virus that causes Acquired Immunodeficiency Syndrome (AIDS). When a person becomes infected with HIV, the virus attacks and weakens the immune system. As the immune system weakens, the person is at risk for getting life-threatening infections and cancers. When that happens, the illness is called AIDS. Once a person has the virus, it stays inside the body for life. According to the Centers for Disease Control & Prevention, AIDS became the leading cause of death for American men aged 25 to 44 in 1992 (www.cdc.gov/mmwr/preview/mmwrhtml/00022174.htm). Two years later, when William was diagnosed with HIV, treatment options were limited a single antiretroviral drug like AZT. With the virus changing or mutating so much, the drugs eventually stop working. A highly successful combination therapy started in 1996. Highly Active Antiviral Therapy (HAART) became the new standard of care for HIV and

greatly lengthened the life span of people living with AIDS. Sadly, William also passed away in 1996, and like many others, never benefited from these new treatment options.

Born in San Francisco, John (he/him) resided there until 1994 when he moved to Portland, Oregon. He traveled the country by RV for 10 years, working remotely at times and taking strange jobs along the way. Working mostly in accounting management, he also took some early forays into floristry, secretarial work, and property management. After spending over 10 years in Tucson, he came back to the Pacific Northwest to enjoy the beauty of the area. This is his first published story.

The Bicoastal Ballad of Sister Inda Beginning

"In the beginning was the Word" John 1:1

By Noah Grabeel

O
n Easter 1979, more than a decade before I was born, a few not-yet-notorious nuns walked the Castro[1]. They wore plain nun habits on loan from a convent under the assumption that the clothes were to be used for a production of the Sound of Music—or so it has been told. Instead, these individuals were on a lark with the simple intention of shaking things up and standing in contrast with the butch leather and denim of San Francisco's famously gay

neighborhood. And what else would you do when suddenly confronted by a nun with a beard as she blesses the fairies and dykes with a rubber chicken? You get on your knees and start confessing.

But then, what is confession for a nun in clown white and drag makeup? While many still are not sure how to react to the spectacle, the original founding of the Sisters of Perpetual Indulgence[2] (SPI) happens to coincide with Michel Foucault's late life exploration of San Francisco's bathhouses and BDSM[3] scene. I can imagine Foucault getting excited about the subversion of confession culture via bearded men in nun drag. One of his most noted works in queer theory, *The History of Sexuality*[4], articulates the church's indoctrination techniques that compel followers to entrust their guilty or perverse thoughts to an authority figure. In many ways, our society has been shaped by the notion that our most ecstatic urges should be handed over to an official who can then help establish or maintain an obedient state. However, those original nuns stumbled upon a community uniquely primed for queer-centered spiritual healing. People confessed their sins, not knowing how else to respond to the iconic nun's habit. The Sisters, still winging it, started the tradition of blessing all who approached. The name of the organization is no mistake either. Indulgences were originally sold by the Catholic church to followers as a means to absolve the sins of their loved ones by getting them out of purgatory so that they could rest in peace in heaven. While Pope Pius V eventually stopped the sale of indulgences, SPI's founding nuns decided to exploit the system by ensuring perpetual get-out-of-purgatory cards for all—free of charge and free from the strictures of organized religion.

That's the mythology, anyway, curated by the Sisters, after 40 years of community service and fundraising. Many aspects of SPI, including its structure, policies, and procedures, have been refined throughout the years, and the Sisters have taken on new responsibilities. The mission of the Sisters touches on all aspects of queer life: to expiate stigmatic guilt and promulgate omniversal joy. Put simply, we celebrate what makes you special while making room for the individuality of others. This mission eventually served as an accessible foothold for my own engagement with the queer community and was the foundation of my personal journey through queer advocacy and self-discovery.

Because SPI is an official grassroots 501(c)(3) organization, these drag nuns must adhere to state regulations to guide and design activities that can offer bespoke aid to emergent, local issues. It would never make sense for an Abbess in San Francisco to mandate activities across the globe for houses in Australia, Germany, France, or the United Kingdom—let alone each United States city or state. The grassroots model helps forward the intent of the organization by putting a focus on direct action and mutual aid. San Francisco's Sisters exemplified this form of community engagement by putting out a safer sex pamphlet and with hospice visits during the AIDS[5] crisis. To this day, sisters continue to advocate for the queer community by providing information and access to condoms, testing kits, medication, and fundraising.

All because some folks got the notion to dress up one Easter morning.

I discovered my own love for dress-up early. As a child, I had access to a collection of costumes, and I spent hours exploring and transforming myself by slipping in and out of different costumes and made-up scenarios. I had no audience and there were no cameras, no Vines[6], not even YouTube. It was just me and my favorite tutus that I kept crammed into a six-foot Rubbermaid bin in a cluttered basement far from any neighborhoods like the Castro. But within that unobserved space, I felt anything seemed possible. Fantastic, idealized versions of myself came to life and multiplied into superheroes and singers and fashionistas. My mother happened to capture this unbridled magic brewing in our home, just 10 miles from the televangelist hotspot—Liberty University. She kept a Polaroid snapshot of my cherubic face on the fridge, my cheeks beaming red, and my smile that knew nothing about restraint. For her and anyone visiting, it was a phase, just silly childhood games. For a while I believed them and thought nothing more of it. That is, until I finally met the indulgent Sisters for myself.

My first encounter with the Sisters happened in Boston at the SPI Convent of the Commonwealth. I had just finished belting out a Jason Robert Brown[7] number for an amateur drag night, the perfect adult sublimation for playing pretend. Performing always fills me with joy; not only from the energy the crowd gives me, but how dynamic I feel when I hold out that last note or nail a tricky, wordy section of a piece.

In the midst of my post-performance high, Sister Lida Christ emerged from a shadowy corner holding a repurposed paint bucket decorated with the word "Donations." She wore a feather boa tacked on to a rhinestone bra and a lace veil cascading off the back. Very much not a wig. I had seen fashion inspirations from Leigh Bowery[8] and others who used unconventional materials in lieu of an updo. But at 25 years old, this was my first encounter with a drag artist who wasn't swept up into RuPaul's Glamazon army. She introduced herself as a clown nun for the local queer community and asked if I'd donate a performance for their yearly grants fundraiser. This was too perfect. I attended that night hoping for this exact scenario: perform and get discovered by another drag queen to get myself booked for her next show. I hoped to kickstart my meteoric drag career and teach the world about gender expansive theory and queer identity.

I worked diligently on my repertoire and decided on an amusing character song from *Wonderful Town*. I was ready. Too ready, in fact. I showed up to the venue just as the bar staff were setting up; not a soul backstage. When the Sisters arrived, I was performance ready and offered to help set up chairs. The room was buzzing with bearded men in dresses wearing sparkling veils, all with bras on their heads. The entire time, I was asking myself," What was all this, and how could I sign up?"

I asked the sisters, and they all echoed the mission of the order in their own words: to spread joy and to erase shame. My goals as a drag performer instantly aligned. I felt a bit silly for the overcomplicated way I had been trying to succeed in the world. I was raised on a steady diet of media and musical theater. I had always viewed success through the mainstream, straight lens of what was marketable, palatable, and comfortable for the general population. These Sisters were none of those things. Their body hair popped out of lace collars and their makeup ranged from classic birthday clown to divine Divine[9]. Even when they interacted with the community, they were doing something I rarely saw drag queens doing in the mid-2010s. Each sister could hold court and still maintain space around them for others to listen, crack jokes, or ask difficult questions. They could easily stop traffic and demand attention at any given moment, but their focus on community engagement was clear as people approached them to satisfy their curiosity, just as I had done.

Setting up for the fundraiser gave me the impetus to change directions. I still wanted bookings for drag performances, but I now wanted to join a group fanatically devoted to uplifting the community through drag and spectacle. I started my initiation into the order immediately following the event. It differs from city to city, but generally takes about a year of dedication to learning how to do as the Sisters do.

During this time, I became more acquainted with Boston's queer community. As much as I was searching for acceptance, I found myself serving as support for other

truth seekers in their own search; folks who had a dream
of something beyond compulsory heterosexuality or mainstream media. Some would try to sneak in their passions by
nervously offering a joking retraction. I recognized in their
tentative confessions that there might be a missing piece in
their life. I often struggled with the worthiness of my own
dreams, and yet it felt so easy and natural to encourage
others. Enough experiences like that with many different
community members, and I began to learn the value of sister
work. Every person struggling to undo years of rejection
inspired me to redouble my own healing work. If the act
of sharing moments of unconditional love with a stranger
strengthened us both, then through regular use, like training a muscle, there was no longer any reason to deny myself
radical grace.

Why shouldn't it be that easy? Wouldn't it be better
if we all just assumed the best intentions and loved every
vulnerable edge of our being? Unfortunately, like anything
worth learning, I felt I had to fight for any gains. In the middle of my initiation into the Sisters, we witnessed the 2016
Election. I was teaching at the time, and I remembered how
apprehensive my class felt about the outcome. I remembered
sharing their fears and reassuring them that level heads
would prevail over all the hate speech and confusion. I also
remembered trying to conduct a class of nervous, despondent college kids after I had slept for only two hours the
night of the election. Not even God herself could sweep into
the classroom and magically fix everything. So, we took time
to process our feelings about the election. Many felt the elec-

tion threatened to overshadow years of advocacy and positive social change for marginalized communities. In the last few months under Obama, I wondered if the Sisters would become irrelevant and fade into obscurity, but the election results refocused my thoughts about how queer folks could continue to flourish despite everything.

I turned to my Sisters for support, and I volunteered my time and energy to host drag bingos and fundraisers. I offered to bless others with a sprinkle of sacred glitter. I strove to make everything OK for myself and others. I tapped into the *sacred fool*, an archetype with a long social history of raising spirits and turning depression into hope. A trickster to make sense of the bleakness. As a Sister is initiated in a local chapter, they slowly add adornments to their nun habit. The public can then start to recognize the presence of a new member on the streets. The recognition brought attention, but on the heels of the 2016 Election, it also brought a more solemn commitment to be visible advocates for each other. Not just being a helper but making a big glittery fuss about lifting up others.

By the time I completed my initiation and my final interview, I felt I had honored the unprecedented history of the Sisterhood by following vows of community service and radical acceptance. Boston's Convent of the Commonwealth carves out space and manifests wonderful queer magic regularly. In my time there, we decorated Valentine cards for isolated queer seniors, rallied for trans youth, and wrapped Christmas presents for families in need. I learned to take action for positive social change, and I no longer waited around for permission to exist. My time in Boston was coming to a close due to grad school and my temp job ending, both in the same month. Everything I learned in the past year gave me the confidence to find my happiness and to encourage others on the same path.

Don't worry. There would be plenty more shenanigans before I could accept that kind of rose-tinted thinking with any consistency. I aimed to do my best, whatever that might look like at the time. I was continually learning to have grace for myself when I was at my lowest. I also had to unlearn trying to make others happy at my own expense. I would shapeshift and conform to stay safe or to gain acceptance. Choosing to express myself as an exuberant drag nun was something no one specifically asked me to do, and that makes me feel pretty powerful.

When I moved out of Boston, I spent the summer relocating to the West Coast and traveling cross country, stopping in with friends along the way. One of my first stops was Louisville, Kentucky, as we celebrated a newly founded SPI chapter for the area. For this special occasion, many Sisters from all over gathered to officially usher in the new nuns. I had done my research and reached out to local Sisters beforehand to make my landing there go smoothly, and I was ultimately relieved to mesh with so many different people so quickly upon arriving.

The superfluity of Sisters buzzed with excitement in a hodgepodge of color, sequins, and clashing apparel. A scene like this might have overwhelmed me in the past—too great a contrast with the black and white world from which I had come. Or maybe the scene would have hit me the way it did that day: with unabashed curiosity. I still felt the same fear of the unknown. That same fear set the backdrop of my travels that summer as I had no idea where I might end up or if I'd even make it as far as the coast. Pushing through the fear made about as much sense to me as putting a bra on my head and asking donors for money. But I learned that, even if everything felt unfamiliar, I could count on my skills and experiences as a Sister to connect with the community and find support wherever I went.

That connection was not always a given. I had grown up in a conservative part of Virginia. Finding a gay person, even a peer in high school, was hard enough, but I was constantly told by my father to be more masculine. I was forced to manage his own insecurities about being discovered as "other" by neighbors and coworkers. I learned to live my life undetected for my father's comfort. I found a new group of cohorts, learning their mannerisms, and curating a persona that won their affection. But I always felt I was playing a survival game. By stark contrast, when I gave others permission to be unfettered, it helped me recognize my own anxieties and realize how irrational they were. I realized connecting with others never had to be so complicated.

Sitting poolside at the end of the Louisville celebration, I watched one of the founders of SPI braid another

Sister's beard hair. After so much time spent thinking about policies, events, and procedures, it was a comfort to see that all our hard work still led to the simplest acts of care. The simplest truths had gotten me this far.

My next stop in the South was Dallas, Texas, where I stayed at one of our larger houses. Despite couch surfing and the fact that my belongings were packed in my Subaru, I kept my veil and nun's habit handy for events. I met up with some Sisters at their local dive bar before meeting with a deaf advocacy group in Cedar Springs, another queer neighborhood. We talked about my cross-country road trip, Louisville's new sister house, and my work in Boston. We got hamburgers at the end of the night and watched people filter in and out of the Round-Up Bar while trading our origin stories.

My favorite part of the Sister's social script is how each of us got started. It varies from person to person in unique and often surprising ways. Despite the international order of SPI being active for more than 40 years, the Sisters still resist mainstream narratives—and for good reason. Summer of 2023 and the spotlight is on the Los Angeles Sisters' relationship with the Dodgers[10] baseball team. It indicates that our striking outfits regularly show up on people's radars, but it is not long before misinformation creeps in or a new trend wipes us from recent memory. Our recruitment strategy is mostly tongue in cheek. My decision to start this path was based on developing my skills and self-exploration, as opposed to blindly doing what others expected from me.

One benefit of this unfettered joining process is understanding my commitment to the order on a purely personal level. Not only who I am, but who I hope to become in the community. Sharing and scrolling through social media can be an exhausting addiction, and I had already spent too much time and energy on figuring out what to post or how to represent my online presence. During my initiation process, I was careful to share my personal experiences only with those closest to me. I was no longer chasing after "likes" or others' approval of my life events. My focus shifted from how all this looked on my resume to redefining my experience in the world. And while this process is unique and deeply personal, each sister's origin story overlaps in this profound way. Whether it is discovering the courage and language to inhabit their true gender identity, finding love, or diving into a new, supportive community, every Sister's history seems to start with that path towards self-actualization. That is when we begin to see the queer wounds inflicted on us by normative society. We see how so many of us survive without the most basic instances of self-care and self-respect in order to meet mainstream expectations.

The Dallas house bucked my own expectations as well. Texas was one of the stops I feared most because I felt it might be comparable to my experiences growing up in Virginia with homophobia and transphobia. Everything I thought I knew about Texas seemed pretty grim, but scrolling through the 30+ Sister faces on the house's website, I was encouraged to walk down Cedar Springs in drag with confidence. After some heavy contemplation, I also discovered my current moniker: Sister Inda Beginning (née Inda Butt), referencing John 1:1 and the importance of the "Word" as a writer.

The name came to me after some lengthy contemplation of my own origin story. While I first saw the Sisters as a stepping stone to a drag career— like idols Sasha Velour[11] and Jinkx Monsoon[12]—the trip had already deepened my connection to the order and unearthed more of my repressed history. So, my name also reflects honoring my upbringing and honoring the child who loved dress-up and was thrilled to bits spending time alone in the basement while wearing a silver disco jumpsuit; honoring my fondest memories of going to my grandma's house, picking out a worn, scarlet nightgown, and fluttering down the hall to paint watercolors of sailboats at her kitchen table; honoring the picture of me wearing my favorite white and red tutu, even as people giggled when they saw it, or wondering why, when I turned 10, my mom suddenly stopped showing it to guests.

I can now transform my inability to conform at an early age into a touchstone for the community. Inda stays curious and asks, "Who did you want to be before someone told you no? In the beginning, who or what did you want to be when anything seemed possible? And what changed?"

For myself, I made sure Inda would always remind me to celebrate my authentic self. As I saw through all the social anxiety and depression of my past, I began to appreciate how I found and shared some spark of my joy each stop along the way. There were still plenty of times I had to "fake it to make it" on my way to the West Coast, but I decided that each step forward would affirm my core truth.

With housing secured and just enough savings to get started in a new city, I left Dallas' southern hospitality and set a course for the Pacific Northwest. My route took me right past Matthew Shepard's[13] hometown of Laramie, Wyoming. I was not convinced of the coincidence until I took an exit that gave me a view of the main street I recognized from Moisés Kaufman's film, Laramie Project[14] I was overwhelmed by the urge to pause on my Sister-fueled pilgrimage. Maybe I could make a quick pit stop and share my journey so far with a local. Maybe someone knew Matthew or maybe his mother would round the corner by some odd chance. I imagined the experiences I would share with her: how her son's cautionary tale in the news cycle kept me alert and cautious and how her family's advocacy and bravery encouraged me to find my light in the darkness and shine it as a beacon for others.

Still, driving by the exit felt more like a glancing blow for Laramie. I powered through the rest of Wyoming, through Boise, and finally got my first dose of five o'clock traffic on I-5 heading for my new home in North Portland.

After years of suggestions that I move somewhere gayer, anywhere queerer, I felt I had finally arrived. Armed with hope of a fresh start and my skills as a sister, I was quick to set up a meeting with the head of membership in the Portland house, the Order of Benevolent Bliss. Sister Donna Vanewday met me to discuss my transition into this new house. It only took a couple cheap drinks before we were swapping eerily similar personal histories and chatting like we were old, childhood friends. As we sat in this neighborhood bar, I felt giddy about joining the fabric of Portland. I saw a variety of gender expressions, body types, and fashion styles that reassured me that I could step outside my fears of the gender binary or having to pass as cisgender male. It blew my mind to see someone with a body like mine—AMAB (assigned male at birth)—fat, hairy, and comfortably chatting at the bar in a sundress. Being a Sister gave me the excuse to do drag on a regular basis. But experiencing the gender diversity in Portland pushed my drag boundaries further than I ever imagined simply by allowing space for my mundane self to develop an affirming, nonbinary wardrobe.

To be fully accepted in the Portland house, I still had to pay my dues and complete a trial period of six months. Yet another whirlwind of introductions, just like Louisville, only it was not just Sisters bringing the magic. Witches, punks, communists, and fierce advocates for progress informed by intersectionality. All of these radical concepts shared a similarly focused vein and were part of the social justice tapestry that I recognized. The naysayers and fearmongers of my past that I once carried with me were soon erased from my inner monologue and replaced with omniversal joy.

And Portland was not lacking in weird universes to explore. One of my first events was a demonstration on

Morrison Street to exorcize the demons of capitalism and compulsory heterosexuality. We helped raise thousands of dollars with Cascade AIDS Project's Art Auction, we recovered lost high heels at the Red Dress party, and we hosted story time performances at the Q Center. I learned more about the local community's needs, and I was thrilled to see that Portland's trans community was not only robust but also a source of support and inspiration for anti-fascism and anti-racism. All of my experiences confirmed that I was right where I needed to be. I made the informed choice of joining the Portland house in 2017.

In the last five years since taking my vows, I have accomplished so much more than I dared to think was possible. I had always dreamed of getting an invitation from my high school as a keynote speaker to address LGBTQ+ history and culture. Imagine my shock reading an email from the Gay/Straight Alliance coordinator inviting me, Sister Inda, to hold a Zoom call for the club's members and faculty support at my old high school in Virginia. In my fantasies, I advocated for acceptance on my old school's front lawn, wearing some spectacular outfit and making a speech that would end hate forever. I closed the laptop on a much quieter experience full of heart. As I cackled and squealed, I was overwhelmed because, not only had I dreamed so big, but I managed to improve on my fantasy by making it real.

I habitually put on clown white and my bravest face and, despite everything, I have become the mentor I never had. It is an honor to share my love for singing at events when called upon or hosting karaoke to encourage others to find their voice. Photos of me as Inda have made it into gallery shows. And here I am getting the chance to write this love letter to the queer community and to write about the most affirming parts of our history. As Inda affirms others, I feel no shame in affirming myself.

In time, I became Vice President in the Portland house, a role that allows me the honor of recruiting and teaching new nuns to join this living piece of queer history. Joining the Sisters was so impactful in changing my life that I selfishly want to lead others through a similar transformation. More importantly, I want to present the opportunity for others to engage in this aspect of queerness that gets less attention than RuPaul's Drag Race or legislatures attempting to police bathroom access. SPI habitually stands up to oppose hate. The founding members in San Francisco published the first affirming safe sex pamphlet during the height of the AIDS crisis. Today, my Sisters and I find ourselves responding to yet another public health crisis with Mpox[15]. Our grassroots efforts strive to forward the queer movement in terms of accessibility and inclusion with online events, remote meetings, and promoting mutual aid.

The vows we take as Sisters may vary from house to house in specific language or meter, but the thrust remains the same. We vow to honor each other's authenticity and hold each other with radical grace and compassion. Nothing is lost in the process. There is plenty of room on this planet for all of us. We can set aside ego-driven judgments to bless others. We can answer complicated questions with empathy and acceptance. We can soothe the callouses that surviving in society gives us. We love, we accept, we adore, we respect. Most of all, we invite anyone in earshot to take these vows with us every year at Pride. SPI has allowed me to define for myself what it means to be a sister and has allowed me space for self-acceptance and visibility. I am no longer stuck in the basement, playing pretend to avoid my father's disapproval. I now share confidence with the passions that drive me. All because I choose to tend the flame that brings me joy, and I continue to dare others to do the same by choosing their joy. So go ahead, close your eyes, click your heels, say the magic words, and let yourself have it.

Endnotes

1 One of the largest gay neighborhoods, in part established by the number of servicemen relocated to the San Francisco area. This neighborhood became a hub of queer culture and boasts many notable residents including Harvey Milk.

2 The Sisters of Perpetual Indulgence® are a leading-edge order of queer and trans nuns. We believe all people have a right to express their unique joy and beauty. Since their first appearance in San Francisco on Easter Sunday 1979, the Sisters have devoted themselves to community service, ministry, and outreach to those on the edges by promoting human rights, respect for diversity, and spiritual enlightenment. We use humor and irreverent wit to expose

the forces of bigotry, complacency, and guilt that chain the human spirit.

3 This abbreviation refers to three related dynamics: B/D (bondage/discipline,) D/s (dominance/submission), and S/M (sadism and masochism).

4 A social history text written by Michel Foucault focusing on the Victorian bourgeoisie culture's influence on shaping sexual history and identity in modernity. Foucault explores the "repressive hypothesis" to understand social influences around sexual activity.

5 From the early 1980s to early 1990s we experienced a significant number of HIV infections and deaths. Our government was criticized for being slow to respond. We saw a surge of activism in large cities across the country despite the backlash of homophobic violence and religious dogma. Brave grassroots organizations like SPI stepped forward to provide education and support when no safety net existed.

6 Launched in 2013, Vine was one of the first social media apps to make the short video accessible to mainstream audiences. These were six-second clips that were played on loop, and those clips were called *vines*. The service was shut down in 2017.

7 American composer, lyricist, and playwright, referenced here for his song. Climbing Uphill, from *The Last Five Years*. Other major works include *Parade, Bridges of Madison County,* and *Songs for a New World.*

8 Australian performer and fashion designer, primarily active in the 80s and 90s. Noted most for his striking outfits and exploration of taboo through clothing.

9 John Waters' film darling and character actor, Divine, AKA Harris Glenn Milstead, challenged more glamorous interpretations of drag to become a punk, cult icon in movies such as *Female Trouble, Pink Flamingos,* and *Hairspray.*

10 During the summer of 2023, Catholic groups urged the Dodgers to uninvite the local Sister chapter to their Pride event.

11 Winner of *RuPaul's Drag Race's* ninth season, who has gone on to produce *Velour Magazine* and the shows *Nightgowns* and *Smoke & Mirrors.* Vocal advocate for drag as an art form and gender theory.

12 Portland darling and winner of *RuPaul's Drag Race: All Stars Season Seven* and sainted by the Portland Sisters as Saint Abby Fab, High Priestess of Heca-THEY, Patron Saint of Gems, Prison Broads, and TARDISes.

13 A gay man from Laramie, Wyoming, who passed due to fatigue and injuries sustained from a hate crime in 1998. Judy Shepard, Matthew's mother, responded to the tragic event by setting up The Matthew Shepard Foundation and inspiring Moisés Kaufman's *The Laramie Project.*

14 Play written by Moisés Kaufman with the Tectonic Theater Project. The piece includes interviews from commu-

nity members and the men responsible for Matthew Shepard's death.

15 Mpox (monkeypox), in the family of variola viruses, was an outbreak in 2022 that prompted raising awareness about getting tested and vaccinated.

Noah (they/them) grew up in Virginia, but moved to Portland, Oregon in 2017. They received an MFA in Creative Writing from Emerson College, where Noah also taught composition and rhetoric. Their work has been featured in Pulp Factor, Nevermore, *and* The Mystery Box Show. *Outside of storytelling, they volunteer with the Sisters of Perpetual Indulgence and take the stage in various drag and musical performances. Noah's favorite animal is the flamboyant cuttlefish.*

Essential Moments: A Journey in Three Parts

By Heidi Bruins Green

I Want to be a Princess: Being seen...Mrs. Gideon, 1968

I **felt invisible as a child.** It's a shadow I've lived in my entire life—classic middle child syndrome. My parents doted on my bright, inquisitive, and strong-willed older sister. My baby brother, the only boy and the family troublemaker, got lots of attention, good and bad. I was the docile one. Obedient, quiet, eager-to-please. Not that I didn't have powerful emotions that roiled through me. Just ask my siblings. I just never felt that anyone was interested enough in me to want to know or care.

Several times, I ran away from home to see if anyone would notice. I didn't actually leave. I hid behind our camping equipment on a high shelf in the garage. I would wait for what seemed like hours for someone to miss me and call for me. No one ever did. Hunger forced me down each time. No one even noticed I'd been gone. I just wanted someone to look for me and fuss over me.

When I was in the second grade, my mom pushed me to be more assertive. She said, "If you act like a doormat, that's how people will treat you." She wanted me to stand up to people who were mean to me or ignored me. But what was I supposed to do exactly? I so much wanted to please her. I just didn't know how.

By 1968, at age 11, I began to think of myself as a feminist. My mom and sister already were feminists, going to NOW[1] meetings (the National Organization of Women). They said feminists were strong and self-sufficient and that I should be, too. Several years earlier, Mom and Dad asked me if I was a feminist. Mom stressed the importance of women's equality and carrying our own weight in the world. Dad talked about the perks of not being a feminist saying, "Men will hold the door open for you, you'll get to go first, you'll be treated like a princess." At 8 years old, being a princess sounded pretty good to me. For several years, Dad and my brother would make a show of opening the car door for me and holding my chair at mealtimes, mostly to irk my mom and sister. At those moments, I felt seen, important, and loved. I didn't understand that I was a pawn in a game with Mom on one side and Dad on the other.

I got glasses in the third grade. I was already taller than everyone in my class, including all the boys. I felt awkward because I wasn't petite and cute like other girls. Glasses!?! None of my classmates had glasses. I couldn't bear to wear them because I thought people would laugh at me for that, too. So, I kept them inside my desk and would sneak them out only when the room was darkened for slides or films.

One day, my kind and beautiful teacher, Mrs. Gideon, quietly got my attention during a movie just after I'd gotten my glasses out. She beckoned me to her desk. She whispered, "Heidi, I see you've gotten glasses. May I see them?" Mortified, I handed her my glasses. I didn't like the attention, though I secretly craved it. Attention could so easily become humiliation. She said in a low whisper, "I love cat-eye glasses! They are so pretty and popular."

I looked at her through my bangs to see if she was mocking me. Her smile was so genuine and warm. At that moment, I felt she really saw me! "I'll bet these are really pretty on you. May I see?" she asked. I nodded and slipped them on. I looked up at her shyly, then stood straighter and brushed my hair back so she could see my face. She silently clapped her hands and whispered, "I knew it! You are such a lovely girl!" Then she breathed, "I know it's scary when people notice something new about you, but go ahead and wear your glasses proudly. They make your eyes so big and shiny." I walked back to my desk and sat down. I don't remember anything about the movie except that I was still wearing my glasses when the lights came on. Now I could see, and now I felt seen.

Being seen by Mrs. Gideon felt like a delicious sip of fresh iced water in my parched throat. People going out of their way to bring me into their circles happened rarely as a kid. I was just "one of" most of the time: one of the Bruins kids, one of the cousins, one of the students, one of the six kids at our church, and on and on. Thanks to Mrs. Gideon's kindness, I felt my confidence blooming. That seemingly small act by Mrs. Gideon let me know I was seen and treasured. I could breathe deeply and be who I was meant to be. Thank you, Mrs. Gideon!

Cue the Lemmings: A Friendship Lost...Diane, 1977

During my second year of college in Santa Cruz in 1977, I attended the concert at which Holly Near[2], a beloved singer of folk and women's music, came out publicly as a lesbian. It was a transcendent moment for the women's community and for me. This woman, whose songs I adored and whose politics reflected and informed my own, was a lesbian! She "looked straight," not like all the lesbians I knew. She had had good relationships with men, but still felt the pull to be with women. I was barely 20 years old, and while I knew I was drawn to women, it only felt like friendship at that time. When Holly Near came out, I saw it as a bold and unequivocal statement of who she saw in the mirror, of who I might someday be.

Holly Near said that coming out was the hardest thing she had ever done. It challenged friends, even in her progressive circles, in ways she did not expect. She said she thought she'd understood what gay people went through coming out, but it was much harder than she had imagined.

She challenged the straight women in the audience— it was a mostly female audience—to come out as lesbians to people in their lives. Even if it wasn't true, she challenged us to experience the terror of possibly losing people close to us. It was to be a test of our friends and ourselves.

Over the next few days, I thought about her challenge. As I examined my attractions, I realized I was not *attracted* to women, but instead, I was drawn to and more comfortable around women than men. It was female-centered political causes that resonated with me. Perhaps I was a "political lesbian?" I reasoned. This logic gave me permission to take on Holly's challenge: I could honestly come out as a political lesbian.

I decided to try it on my high school best friend, Diane. I planned to stay with her and her family for a few weeks over the summer while I looked for an apartment. Since my mom's death the year before, they had stepped up in many ways. I felt secure in Diane and in her family's love for me. Truthfully, I'd always felt that Diane liked me a bit more than I liked her. She made all the initial overtures, and she'd pursued my friendship. Her clear interest made me feel safe. We stayed at each other's houses on the weekends and talked on the phone most evenings during high school.

Arriving at their home at the beginning of summer, I gathered my courage and launched into Holly Near's challenge. I told Diane that I was a political lesbian. I slipped it smoothly into the conversation as if it were a common, well-understood term. (It never was and even now doesn't have the meaning I gave it).

It did not go well. All Diane heard was "lesbian." Instantly, the conversation became heated. Diane accused me of being perverted and said, "Santa Cruz twisted your mind and made you sick." I continued on as if "political lesbian" was a normal thing to say in the 1970s, and I ignored the fact that I had provoked an emotional firestorm in Diane. I logically replied that since the causes I cared about were all focused on women's issues, it made sense to call myself a "political lesbian." I didn't *say* I was attracted to women, but I didn't *say* anything about still being attracted to men, either. I felt that would be cheating on Holly Near's challenge.

That small bit of information might have saved my friendship with Diane. Maybe not, though, since I couldn't say I *wasn't* attracted to women. I didn't know the term "bisexual" at the time. That might have been a moot point anyway. I don't think Diane would have felt reassured by that term either.

The last thing Diane said to me was, "What would your dead mother think?" She stormed out of the house to go see her boyfriend, Ed.

Diane's immediate reaction hurt me. I was also righteously indignant when telling and re-telling others about what I saw as her homophobia and betrayal in the years that followed that summer. But in the nearly 50 years since, I've realized that I was at fault for springing this on my best friend as a "test." I used my word choices to mislead her. It didn't occur to me that she would have issues about me being gay. I thought she would laugh and ask, "What does 'political lesbian' even mean?" and I would unpack the construction. But it was the 70s, and she was very religious. She felt uncomfortable, maybe even threatened. We had been best friends throughout high school. I realize now that I had set her up, and I should have anticipated her response. In hindsight, her reaction was not a surprise.

Much later, I realized that Holly Near's challenge may have been rhetorical. Perhaps she was asking us to *imagine* what would happen rather than to actually engage in a deception that could have devastating consequences.

I've only seen Diane once in the many years since then. It was eight years later at our 10-year high school reunion. We had a single, brief conversation. She was still furious with me. I admitted to her what I said was an experiment, and that I hadn't been totally truthful at the time—although at that point, I did identify as a lesbian and had a girlfriend. I apologized for confusing Diane. We agreed to meet the next day to talk it over, but she never showed up. She never answered my phone calls. She has avoided all my other attempts at contact. I even looked for her on Facebook and couldn't find her.

The one good thing that came out of losing my friend, Diane, was that it transformed how I communicate my truth to other people. Now, every time I share my truth, I first make sure it *IS* true and that communicating it clearly with other people is a necessity. I use language designed to meet people where they are and that makes my meaning clear. Then I listen with an open heart and all my senses to their reaction.

Five years after losing my friendship with Diane, I used what I learned from that experience when I came out for real as a lesbian. I used this approach again when I came out as bisexual 15 years later while I was still exclusively with women. And again after 10 more years when I fell in love with a man. I lost friends at each juncture—losing the most when I married my husband, Jamison—but I never again lost a friend because I was callous or careless. Diane taught me that even the strongest bonds can break if you treat them with disregard. Diane, wherever and however you are, I still love you, and I regret the pain I caused you. And I will always remember to live by the valuable lesson you taught me.

My People:
An Enduring Friendship...
Stephanie, 2022

On November 1, 2022, I received a mass email from her children saying that Stephanie, my best friend for 47 years, had died on Halloween. First, shock and grief, then a chasm of shame opened up to devour me. I knew she was battling breast cancer, but how did I not know my best friend was about to die? Why had I not been on the phone with her in the days before her death? Why hadn't I known her death was imminent and flown down to be with her? Not just then but in the preceding months as her health went downhill. From what she told me, I thought she was getting better. How could I dare call myself her best friend and not realize what was really happening behind her words? In the months since her death, I've gingerly explored that yawning gulf and tried to come to terms with the impact of her death and her life on me.

The fall of 1975, when I was 18, was the first time I encountered Stephanie, one of "my people." We instinctively know who "our people" are, whether through pheromones for lovers or the feeling that someone is a kindred spirit in powerful friendships.

I arrived at my dorm room on move-in day at college. Stephanie's room was two doors down, and she was a force to behold. People were clustered outside her door as she held them enthralled with her wicked-smart wit. My reaction to her was instant and visceral. I felt my whole body say, "She's going to be my best friend." What my body didn't say, or I didn't realize for several years, was that it was also love at first sight. Spoiler alert: Stephanie and I never became lovers, though we were in love with each other at different times. Ultimately, I believe this was a good thing. As lovers, we would have burned hot and bright and ended explosively, shattering the bond of friendship we shared for nearly five decades.

At Stephanie's funeral, I met dozens of people who were also drawn to her energy, passion, and intellect. I'd never met most of them, although I recognized many of their names. Upon meeting me, many people said, "Oh, you're Stephanie's Heidi!" Then they'd say Stephanie often shared outrageous stories from our college days or our later adventures.

The truth was that Stephanie and I had lived very separate lives since college, mostly connecting by phone, letters, and later email. We were rarely in the same space physically, except to meet for occasional girls' weekends away. That said, I was right all those years ago when I stood at my dorm room door and made my prediction: we did become best friends and remained so until the end. We counted ourselves as both soulmates and kindred spirits.

Stephanie had been receiving treatment for breast cancer for 18 months when she died suddenly that Halloween (her favorite holiday). Her death seemed sudden because

I didn't realize how sick she was. The last time we'd spoken, several months earlier, she talked about how well her treatment was going. She regaled me with funny stories about her misadventures at the clinic in Los Angeles. She shared tales about her two children, of whom she was justifiably proud, and about irritating encounters with her ex-husband or his new wife. All were described with Stephanie's signature disarming, self-deprecating, and biting humor.

We laughed. We also talked about serious matters. But mostly, we laughed. I didn't know that was the last time I would connect with my first true soulmate.

Stephanie and I spent the first two years of college together at the University of California, Santa Cruz (UCSC). From the beginning, we became fast friends and shared a number of mutual friends. We all joked and competed to see who could tell the funniest story or deliver the most outlandish comeback line.

On March 2, 1976, during my first year of college, my mother died suddenly of a massive cerebral hemorrhage. That morning, I learned she had been in a coma since the night before. After tracking down my sister, who also attended UCSC, we left within the hour, hoping to get home in time to say goodbye. We were 300 miles away. It was winter—impassable snow. Mom died before we got home, before we even got on the plane. I returned to school a month later at the beginning of the spring quarter.

At that age, most of us didn't know how to talk about death, so my friends and I fell back into our superficial, joking conversations. I felt cast adrift, and my heart was shattering every moment, but it was easier to make a mindless joke than to talk about the raw emotions surrounding my mother's death.

A few weeks later, I was sitting in the dorm hallway at 2 a.m., joking with Stephanie and our friend, Alison, when I broke down. I could no longer bear the pain silently. I asked Stephanie and Alison if we could talk seriously about my mom's death. This was a breach of young adult protocol, and we all awkwardly held our breath. Then they both leaped in with hugs and words of reassurance. They had wanted to talk but didn't know how to ask. I sobbed as they held me. I talked about my mom, what she'd meant to me, and how I didn't know how to navigate the world without her. They revealed that my mom's sudden death had scared them and how they feared this could also happen to their own moms. My friendship with Stephanie shifted that night. It took on a closeness forged in tragedy. She saw the real me and, rather than reject me, gathered me into her arms and her heart. I recognized that her quick jokes hid her own vulnerability and revealed a kindred fear of rejection. She had serious issues she needed to share, too, and she had no more skills than I did. We tacitly established a no-bullshit policy that night.

When she dropped out of college after our second year to move to San Francisco, we saw each other frequently. I would drive the hour to the Bay Area for a fun weekend, and we'd relax into the bond between us. We went to Mexico for a month between my third and fourth years of college.

We went to Europe together for three months after I graduated from college and just before she went to UC Berkeley.

She lived in the Bay Area for another decade, and we continued to see each other often. I moved to Davis with a man I thought I would marry. Six months later, I left him when I fell in lust (which I mistook for love) with a woman named Debbi.

Stephanie saw me through it all as my world expanded. She shared my brief triumphs and my crushing heartaches, and she watched me repeatedly fall for Debbi's protestations of fidelity. Stephanie even met, loved, and lived with a woman for a year, further bonding us as we explored being "women-loving women." Stephanie had good taste in women. I, obviously, still needed to develop discernment.

Then Stephanie met a man, fell in love, and moved to Los Angeles with him.

For the first 10 years that Stephanie lived in LA, I drove down from Davis regularly to spend the weekend with her. That also meant spending time with her boyfriend, Chris. His politics were a little to the right of Genghis Khan. He called me a flaming liberal. He and I would bicker and snipe the whole weekend. Stephanie agreed he was an ass but swore he had other charms. I told myself before each trip that I would not talk politics with him, but it never worked. Looking back, I think he was jealous of me. He didn't understand, or maybe feared, the power of Stephanie's relationship with me.

Several times after Stephanie and Chris married, Stephanie and I went away for a few days to a cottage in Monterey, California. Heavenly times. The drive to Monterey was equal distance for both of us; we could be ourselves rather than someone's wife or girlfriend. It was like taking a deep breath of fresh air.

Over time, Stephanie's life got busier. Teaching at a private school was demanding, and Stephanie was a gifted and devoted teacher. After her children were born, she got so busy that having overnight guests was difficult, and getting away for a weekend was impossible. But we often shared hours-long gabfests by phone to stay in touch. We continued our long-distance friendship over the decades. Sometimes months passed between our calls. But when we picked up the phone, we picked up right where we left off.

After Stephanie finally divorced her cheating, gaslighting spouse, we called each other much more often. Our calls were like precious gems to me, a time-out with "my person," the one who really saw me. I could be myself with Stephanie. She shared her world with me through those calls, and together we dove deeply into mine. That connection was a balm to both our souls.

At Stephanie's funeral, I learned that many people who came from near and far were as shocked as I was at the email announcing her death. People said, "I just talked to her, and she seemed fine!" "She just told me a funny story the other day." "We hadn't talked for a while, but I had no idea the cancer was worse."

Her daughter, Kelsey, provided the hidden piece of the puzzle with her remarks during the service, "Mom was private about her health, for all that she was the life of the party and lived life out loud. The greatest gift you could give her was a conversation where you laughed together. Serious health issues had no place there for her."

"The day she died, Halloween, she woke up short of breath. That was her only symptom. Even that didn't stop her from joking with us all day long.

"Toward evening, when she wasn't feeling better, we took her to the hospital. In the ambulance, she had me laughing at a story I'd never heard about her most risqué Halloween costume back in college."

I remember that costume; Stephanie was Nanuck of the North, wearing a short, barely-covering-her-ass fur parka, cowboy boots, and literally nothing else.

"After examining her, the doctor said he had no immediate concerns, except that her blood oxygen was low, so he would put her on oxygen and monitor her overnight. He suggested we go home for a good night's sleep and return in the morning."

Kelsey's eyes filled with fat, shiny tears, her voice suddenly softer, breaking.

"The doctor told me that after we left, he went out of the room for two minutes to get the nurse to set up the oxygen, and when they came back, she was gone. Just...gone. He never expected that. No one knew she would just be gone."

Kelsey's brother, Drew, put his arm around her. She buried her face in his shoulder, and they stepped away from the pulpit.

That's how my dearest friend—my touchstone, my person, the one who still owns a huge chunk of my heart—slipped away.

My friendship with Stephanie endured despite the limitations of time and distance that separated us physically. We were comfortable in our occasional reconnections. We truly saw and cherished each other. We were in each other's hearts, and that was enough to pick up right where we'd left off. All the same, with the loss of Diane's friendship and the death of my person, Stephanie, I have made a vow in Stephanie's memory: to always hold close the precious jewels of my friends. And, like Mrs. Gideon, to let them know I see them for who they are, that they matter to me, and to tell them how much I appreciate and treasure them.

Endnotes

1 The National Organization for Women (NOW) was founded in 1966 and is the largest organization of feminist grassroots activists in the United States with 550 chapters in all 50 states and over 500,000 members. NOW faced many criticisms, especially in its early years, for being focused on

the rights of straight, White, liberal (vs. radical), privileged women. In working to address those valid criticisms, NOW has been a powerful force for change in US society.

The NOW chapter in Bakersfield, California, where I grew up, led "consciousness-raising" sessions to help women (and girls) better understand and articulate the rights and opportunities that we were being denied and how to fight for those rights. My mom took my sister to meetings for a year before taking me. Initially, it was hard for me to see what being "a princess" really entailed. Once I did, I asked my mom to buy me a necklace with a women's symbol with a fist in the center to help me remember to hold my power. I wore that necklace for many years to remind myself to be the woman I was growing up to be.

2 Holly Near is a singer-songwriter, teacher, and activist born in Ukiah, California. Holly Near was and is one of the earliest and brightest stars of a genre called "women's music" within feminist circles and lesbian/ bisexual+ women's communities. A type of folk music, "women's music" celebrates the power of women taking collective action to make social change. It also celebrates relationships between wom-

en-loving-women (lesbian and bisexual women in same-sex relationships).

Holly Near's music was a powerful force in my life, and I felt she'd been where I was in both her sexuality and her activism. She cares about the planet and about national and international politics. When she came out as a lesbian, I still felt straight. But as a Women's Studies major, I was queer-adjacent. Holly showed me the path I knew deep down I needed to follow. When 10 years as a lesbian didn't quite fit me anymore, Holly had already shifted to identifying as bisexual (I also went to a concert where she talked about that shift in her desires and consciousness). Holly Near's music is compelling, powerful, and well worth spending some time with.

Heidi (she/her) is a social justice advocate. She believes that changing hearts and minds involves persuading people to expand their awareness beyond their own stories. She has championed LGBTQ+ issues in the workplace for the last 40+ years. In 2013 she was invited to the White House to present evidence of bisexual+ plus workplace disparities. Heidi continues social justice work today.

Essential Moments: A Journey in Three Parts

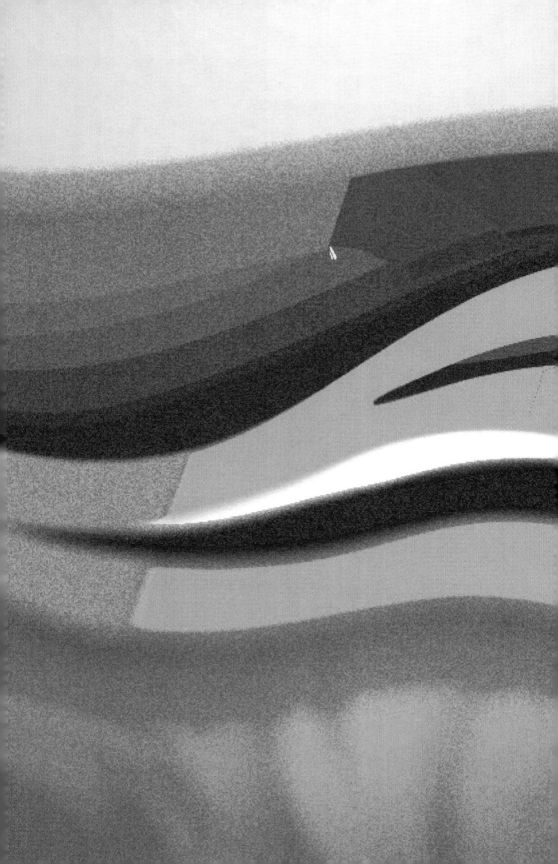

Vestigial

A very small remnant of something that was once more noticeable

By Jonanna Widner

Here's something you should know about me: my bladder is roughly the size of a squirrel's paw.

I mean it. I go to the bathroom 11, 12, 13 times a day. I've practically worn a path in the carpet between my couch and my bathroom.

For many people, this would be a minor inconvenience at worst. Maybe it's just one of those weird body things we all have, like one nostril being slightly larger than the other or a vestigial nipple. And in my own house, it's merely that. The vestigial nipple of my life. The ol' triple nipple.

But the thing is: using a public restroom is an entirely different story.

Almost every single time I enter a women's restroom, another woman in there freaks out. Sometimes it's a minimal freakout—their eyes widen slightly for a split-second before their brains do the math. Then they relax and, with a little lowering of the eyebrows, they scoot out. Sometimes it's worse. Sometimes they stare. Sometimes they look angry. Sometimes—many times—they literally say, "This is the *women's* bathroom."

Part of me understands. I am fully aware of what I look like. I am a woman on the inside, but on the outside I look like a guy—specifically, the Verizon guy from the commercials. And for thousands of years we've taught ourselves that a woman isn't supposed to look like the Verizon guy— or any other guy for that matter. But a lot of us do. That's the thing.

There is a particular type of bathroom person, the kind that makes my heart crumple. These are the ones who look aggressively startled, flopping backwards like a Muppet who's been shot. Once on the Nike campus a lady opened the bathroom door to enter just as I was leaving. She Muppet-flopped, turned and looked at the "W" on the door, then turned and looked at me. She turned and looked at the "W" again, then turned and looked at me *again*. She was preparing to turn a third time when I finally growled, "You're in the right place." And then I grabbed a fist full of free tampons and jammed them in my bag to prove that I, too, have a vagina. But my bag was a completely androgynous black backpack, so it didn't really help. Whatever.

The point is, I go through this every single time I go to a public bathroom. It's stressful. It hurts. It feels like being in another country and not speaking the language. Like France, I guess. And I wish I didn't, but I feel so ashamed about it. Using the restroom is a basic human routine that most people do on autopilot. But for me, that first "I gotta pee" metastasizes into "fuck, I'm going to have to go into that bathroom." I feel a swirl of apprehension whenever I leave my seat at work and walk across the room to the restroom. "Please don't let anyone be in there. It would be so much easier," I tell myself. By the time I reach the door, little squirts of adrenaline are having a dance party in my stomach. And deep down there it is—unearthed—that tiny piece of internal shame that I haven't quite conquered. And I don't feel like I ever will.

Every time: at a Blazers game, at the airport, at work, at the Nike store, at the coffee shop, at the gym, at the grocery store, at the movies, at the pizza place, at the concert, at the bookstore. At the airport. Especially the airport. Every time.

So when the squirrel's paw calls to me, it's an alarm bell. It reminds me that in a few seconds, I will put my hand on the door marked with a "W," and on the other side someone might be there. She might do nothing. She might look at the floor. Or she might muppet-flop, stop in her tracks and panic. And I'll be forced to reassure her, "You're in the right place."

And that little dark shadow of shame grows two-fold because it shouldn't matter to me that it matters to me. So now I'm ashamed about the shame. It's really a lot when all I want to do is go pee in a public restroom and have my biggest concern be holding in my farts just like any other person. So yeah, it still matters to me. And I think about why it does all the time.

Maybe the bathroom stuff wouldn't matter as much to me if this whole dynamic didn't permeate most interactions in my life. I bust people staring at me all the time. I'm not joking. All. The. Time. I'm pretty sure they aren't doing it because they think I'm the Verizon guy. I get weird looks in the women's department because why would a guy be shopping for sports bras? I get weird looks in the men's department because why would a woman need a tie? I get double-taked, sneered at, and whispered about on a daily basis. I expect it in the Bible Belt where I'm from. But it still happens in Portland, and those times sting the most. Y'all are supposed to be the ones who have your progressive shit together! I'd like to be able to blow it off, and usually I do. But also, I'm a human being, and sometimes it really chips away at me. Sometimes it goes deeper. My mom died almost exactly two years ago, early February, and I heard the whispers even then.

My mom died of a totally random and rare cancer that tricked her body into emitting hormones that gave her stomach flu-type symptoms every single day. Her body could barely retain any nutrition, so she just got skinnier and skinnier. It was a long and terrible battle for her. It was so day-to-day that I almost got used to it. But in the end, it was terrible to watch. I can't imagine what it was like for her.

She was in and out of hospitals, and the hospital where she died was beautiful. A teaching hospital in Dallas, Texas, with an entire floor full of soothing, modern paintings. The waiting areas had comfy padded chairs with those vaguely modern, geometric upholstery patterns. The steel and glass elevator glided so smoothly it felt like you weren't even moving. You just got in and a few seconds later you were transported someplace slightly different than where you were before.

A few days before she died, I was in that elevator alone going to the sixth floor. The door opened and a young mom and her little kid got on. I'm sure I was a mess. We got to my mom's floor and right then the kid said, "Mommy, is that a boy or a girl?" The door opened and the mom said, "I don't know." I got off and walked down the hall, opened the door to my mom's room, and forgot about it for a while. I had other pain to deal with.

I understand where the kid was coming from. It's not the kid's fault. That kid was doing their best to understand something that didn't jibe with the big pile of a calcified tradition that dictates how we all see the world. Seeing me must have been like a record skipping. And normally I would celebrate that "I don't know." Living in the "I don't know" zone allows me to see the world in ways most people don't, and I am so grateful for that. I feel lucky.

But sometimes the "I don't know" comes at a time when you're in a starkly beautiful building and your mom is dying. And it's a lonely place to be. That's when "I don't know" doesn't feel like a celebration of who I am; it feels like just a phrase used to erase who I am. It's another moment when it shouldn't matter, but it matters a lot to me.

But there is so much hope, right? Every time I see a bathroom sign that signifies all sorts of genders, I want to hug the person in the next stall. Any time I see a bathroom sign that says, "Whatever—just wash your hands," I think, "Yes! Now we're getting to the real problems in our society." (Y'all really need to wash your hands!) Any time a straight ally offers to come with me to the restroom, even though they themselves just went, just so I feel more comfortable— well, sometimes I kind of want to cry. Picture me tearing up at the paper towel dispenser and a stranger asks, "Are you ok?" and my response is, "I'm more OK than you know."

It's those things that slay my shame demons—that remind me queer people aren't just the weird anomalies that much of the world thinks we are. We are people just like anyone else with all the usual stuff that means something. We have bodies and brains just like anyone, and jobs and dogs and favorite beers and lives with all sorts of struggle and love and fun. We have families and dear ones, nieces we cheer on, and boyfriends we adore. And sometimes moms we mourn. So, I ask you: if someday you're in an elevator, and you see someone who looks like me, and your kid asks, "Is that a boy or a girl?" Go ahead and say, "I don't know, honey." Just make sure and add, "But it doesn't matter."

Jonanna (she/her) was born and raised in Fort Worth (and now happily a Portlander). Jonanna started her career as a high school sports writer in small-town Texas, which was a real trip because it was exactly like Friday Night Lights. She's done a ton of sportswriting and was a music editor at two different alt-weeklies back when alt-weeklies were a thing. When they weren't a thing anymore, she switched to advertising. Also she hates writing about herself in the third person.

Misfit to Mensch

By Paul Iarrobino

When I was 6 years old, our family moved from a crowded flat on a busy street to a newer tract home in a quieter Boston neighborhood. Our new digs were huge in comparison. Four bedrooms. Three bathrooms. A finished basement. A big backyard and lots of neighborhood kids our age to play with.

How my mother held things together I will never know. My father worked long shifts as a union bricklayer. He was our provider but was often gone for long stretches. My stay-at-home mom had her hands full trying to raise six kids with little emotional support.

Looking back on it now, our loud, working-class, "Eye-a-talian" family didn't fit the more subdued, white-collar, Irish neighborhood. We did have Catholicism in common, but how we practiced it varied greatly from our more affluent neighbors. My earliest memories of Catholicism were steeped in hypocrisy. Although my parents never went to church, we kids were supposed to attend regularly. But my older brothers and sisters had other ideas. I tagged along with them as they passed right by St. Theresa's Church, continued up Centre Street, and entered the steamy, sweet goodness of Anna's Hand Cut Donut shop. I knew telling a fib to our parents was wrong, but I was sworn to secrecy. Our family's collection box money was spent on mouth-watering donuts. My favorites were the frosted chocolate crullers and the honey dips. Before we left, we wiped the sugary glazes off our faces and inspected each other for any evidence. To document our attendance at church, we were required to bring home the church bulletin as proof. My older siblings usually ordered me to go into the church foyer to retrieve the bulletin.

Speaking of Catholicism: true confession...I had an afternoon addiction. Every day after school, I headed to our quiet, cool basement where I had a lot of privacy. My siblings were outside playing with the neighborhood kids. My mother was upstairs busy caring for a new infant and trying to get our family's dinner started. I had plenty of time to myself in the basement to entertain my afternoon addiction: watching my favorite TV show, *Dark Shadows*.

We had an extra black and white TV in the basement, and it was my saving grace. At 4 p.m., I would turn on Dark Shadows. At 6 years old, I didn't understand the storyline, but I was mesmerized by Barnabas and eventually Quentin. I was too young to understand why the men captured my attention, let alone talk to anyone about it.

Once a week after school, I was supposed to attend catechism at St. Theresa's Church. Yes, the same church where we pulled the weekly bulletin and turned it over as evidence of our attendance. This was in preparation for my first holy communion. My older siblings explained the charade to me. All I had to do was memorize three prayers, show up at church for the ceremony, and wear white. My large extended family would then come to our home and celebrate my first holy communion. There would be a big Italian feast with cake and lots of gifts—especially cash. Easy-breezy.

I decided to watch *Dark Shadows* instead of attending weekly indoctrination sessions. I even created a foolproof option: home study. I would memorize the required prayers during commercials. I had the weekly deception covered.

Everything was going to plan. Then, one day, something unexpected rocked my young world. I came home from school and slunk into the basement as usual. When I turned on the TV, *Dark Shadows* was not on. What? I changed all *three* stations, and a news event interrupted all the regular programming. A man was landing on the moon. So what?! Why couldn't they cover it later during the evening news?! I looked at my glow-in-the-dark *Dark Shadows* watch and decided it was time I made an appearance at catechism. I bolted to St. Theresa's Church, having attended only one class, and I hoped to discreetly seat myself.

I got there a few minutes late, sweaty from running and heart pounding. There, standing in front of the classroom, was Sister Moniece. Our eyes locked. She waved me with her hand to the front of the room. All eyes were on me as I nervously walked down the middle aisle and approached the front of the room. It felt like the parting of the sea. Sister Moniece pointed to the seat directly in front of her. No surprise, it was vacant. I sensed the class feared her, but I didn't know why. It's not like I had much experience with church other than sneakily retrieving the bulletin on Sundays.

Just as I sat down, Sister Moniece asked me to please stand. As I started to stand, I could foresee the game unfolding. My siblings had coached me enough to know she was going to quiz me on prayer memorization. Even though I didn't know what the prayers meant, I knew I had completely mastered my home study during commercials.

"Hail Mary, full of grace, hallowed be thy name..."

"Our father who art in heaven..."

It was like a kid's version of a Shakespearean play.

But no, Sister Moniece had other plans for me that day. And I was not prepared for what was about to happen.

Sister Moniece asked me why I decided to bless the class with my presence on this particular day.

I was caught off guard. My young mind was still reeling about missing a *Dark Shadows* episode.

"I usually watch my favorite show, *Dark Shadows*, but some guy landed on the moon, and they put it on all the TV stations. So, I decided to come here today instead since I had nothing else to do."

The entire classroom erupted in laughter. I saw Sister Moniece's face turn bright red. I was mortified. I had no idea what was so funny. Was it something I said?!

While her technique of using guilt and shame on me didn't exactly go as planned, it did work in terms of getting me to cut my Dark Shadows viewing habit on Tuesdays—but only until I made my first holy communion. After that, I watched faithfully until 1973. I was 11 years old when Dark Shadows was slated for cancellation. Despite our loyal fan club's avalanche of letters to ABC, we lost our battle to save the show.

I missed watching Dark Shadows. I slowly updated my viewing habits to include PBS's Zoom; a program designed for kids by kids, not the modern-day ZOOM online platform.

"Come on and Zoom, Zoom, zooma-Zoom.

We're gonna zooma zooma zooma-ZOOM!"

It was filmed in Boston, and I secretly hoped to be one of the Zoom kids. They even encouraged viewers to submit their interest by snail mail.

"Send it to Zoom, Box 350, Boston MA 02134, send it to Zoom!"

But those kids seemed so confident and well-adjusted. I was sure they didn't hide in their dark basements alone watching gothic soap operas. I never mailed them about my interest in being a Zoom kid, despite secretly rehearsing in my basement.

Also around this time, I realized I was attracted to members of the same sex. Boys weren't supposed to have crushes on other boys. Now I understood why I had had full-on crushes on Barnabas and Quentin, the characters on Dark Shadows. I learned it was called homosexuality. Such an odd word. Trips to the local library card catalogs led me to dusty research books. I soon learned that in clinical terms I was Sick. Abnormal. Pathological. Deviant. Something I needed to be cured of. I didn't know anyone like me, and I was convinced I was the only one.

Since I was already good at keeping secrets, I kept this to myself, too. With the lack of role models and from over-hearing conversations in my working-class neighborhood, I knew I was destined for a pathetic, short life. My career choices and places to live would be limited. How could such dark and lonely prospects be my future?!

In my neighborhood, people created nicknames, and my family was very good at it. Some of those nicknames were brutal and stayed with people for years. Our tomboy neighbor, Marge, who excelled at sports, was called Marge the Barge. Johnny, who had two large front teeth, was called

Chipmunk. I had my own share of nicknames. During puberty, I grew one foot in one year, and I was sleeping a good 12 hours a day. My family nicknamed me the Sleeping Giant, based on the iconic frozen food Jolly Green Giant. You may remember him. "Ho, Ho, Ho, Green Giant." Ho, Ho, Ho, The Sleeping Giant!

Once my 12-year-old-self realized I had limited career choices due to stereotypes, I decided to become a hairdresser. I offered haircuts in my backyard. It turned out I couldn't even succeed as a homosexual-in-training. I gave God-awful, embarrassingly uneven haircuts. Neighborhood mothers complained, and my mom was then forced to revoke my cutting shears. My early admission to cosmetology school was out of the question. Now what?

It was during my haircutting days that my siblings nicknamed me MOP. It didn't seem as bad as some of my other nicknames. I figured it had to do with my long, stylish hair and my desire to cut hair.

I found out one day by accident that it wasn't why they nicknamed me MOP. I heard my older siblings laughing behind a closed door. After they left, I discovered a crumpled piece of paper in the trash can. MOP was actually an acronym. It stood for Mental Oddball Paul. Ouch! My spirit was broken, I felt crushed and so alone as I watched more movies and TV in the basement and retreated further into myself.

My home life became a required necessity. I developed an entrepreneurial spirit by delivering newspapers, babysitting, cutting grass (not hair!), shoveling snow, or washing windows. If I could save enough money, I figured I could find a way to leave home, even if the details were sketchy at best. Besides, I enjoyed being responsible, helping people, and being validated by others. Earning money allowed me to buy my own clothes. I was determined not to wear my brother's less stylish hand-me-downs. Let's be real. I became a fashion icon during my teen years. And I had the feathered hair to go with it!

Going to high school was pure torture for me. I was one year behind my brother who was a popular jock. He played every sport imaginable and made friends easily. Then there was me. With my height, certainly I could play basketball, right?! Not a chance!

My main focus during high school was plotting my escape. I knew I needed to leave home. But how? College was a great excuse. I realized I was on my own emotionally and financially. I had my sights set on any state college that was at least two hours away from home.

I was beyond excited when I received my acceptance letter from University of Massachusetts at Amherst. My father was disappointed. He wanted me to live at home and commute to a local university to save money. But he didn't know what was deep in my heart. I knew I had to leave home to truly discover who I was and to learn what I could become in this world.

During my sophomore year, I began to find myself. I was selected as a resident assistant (RA), and I had my own room. This afforded me privacy and a whole new peer group of other RAs. We were a supportive, accepting bunch and we also helped each other solve conflicts that occurred on our respective floors.

It was during this time that I questioned my narrow world view and examined issues with curiosity—everything from racism to vegetarianism, feminism to political protests. As RAs, we received a lot of social issues training. We were well-informed and able to support any of our peers who were in crisis.

This is when I learned about the PGA. Not to be confused with the golf tournament, PGA stood for the People's Gay Alliance, one of the sanctioned student clubs on campus. I occasionally walked by their office, but I was always too afraid to go inside. Someone might recognize me!

I heard about a monthly PGA dance at the campus center. It just sounded so...scandalous...to me. Would people be watching to see who came and went? I was fearful, but my curiosity was growing.

Little by little, I felt I could safely express my feelings to my left-leaning peer group. The fact that I was gay was really no big deal to them. It was like being a vegetarian or a Unitarian Universalist[1] or an environmentalist. It was truly a non-issue. I enjoyed this new freedom and this more positive outlook of my future.

I finally got the nerve to go to one of the dances. I spent hours picking out the right outfit. I wore black and white, pinstripe pants, a white dress shirt, and a blazer I rescued from a vintage clothing store. I rolled up my sleeves, shined my black dress shoes, and slicked my hair back with gel.

I went with a group of friends so I wouldn't feel so alone. They served drinks and played upbeat dance music. It was magical. I lost myself in the music, and I saw the place come alive. I felt so free dancing with friends, even if we were only allowed to do so for a few hours once a month.

After graduation, I worked human service jobs in Boston. The wages were low, and the rents were prohibitively expensive. I vacationed in the Northwest in my mid-20s. And, when I returned home, I remembered how laid-back Portland, Oregon, was.

The people in Portland seemed so relaxed and friendly. They didn't appear as hardened as the people in Boston. There were these weird anomalies. People actually stood on the escalators. There wasn't a slow and fast escalator lane like I was used to in Boston. Drivers didn't honk their horns because that wasn't polite. Bus passengers thanked their bus driver. And grocery store clerks asked how you were doing. But, best of all, Portland's housing was dirt cheap compared to Boston.

So, at the age of 27, I moved to Portland, Oregon. I immediately fell in love with this quirky city with its green spaces and polite people. I enjoyed the more relaxed way of working and living there. This was the fresh start I craved and a chance to live my life more authentically.

Portland definitely agreed with me. I found work right away and was able to buy a house within two years. I spent my 30s and 40s comfortably nesting, making new friends, continuing my work in human services, and spending several years in a long-term relationship.

During my mid-40s things started to change. I found myself working for the same organization but in a more stressful role. I was also newly single after many years, and I was not finding much joy in my life.

After a few rounds of unsuccessful dating, I met someone new online, my now-husband, Arnel. We talked for several days before meeting in person during a major snowstorm. We had strong feelings for each other, but early on there was a problem: he wasn't out. I was the first man he was with, and I knew I could no longer keep secrets like this ever again. It took me a long time to get to a place where I lived my life openly. I was not about to budge. I was not stepping backwards into the closet.

We continued our conversations about his fears of coming out. I understood Arnel's situation. Unlike me, he actually liked his family and wanted their approval. He was tired of well-intentioned coworkers trying to fix him up with women. I understood the loneliness that led him to placing an online profile. There was a lot at stake for him. I knew coming out was ultimately a decision he would need to make. I was thrilled when he told me he wanted to try, but he didn't know how and when. He sought my advice.

I thought about it for a second and said, "Well, it's January now...let's just say I will be having dinner with your family on Thanksgiving, so you figure it out!"

Being the rational one, Arnel applied his expert project management skills to the challenge and made deadlines for himself. In March, I met a few of his close friends. He then made a bold move by inviting me to meet his large extended family at their annual July 4th barbecue. He probably thought this casual outdoor gathering would be an ideal opportunity for me to meet his family for the first time. This would surely make Thanksgiving a breeze, I thought. I just love logical people!

His Filipino family, like my Italian family, value an abundance of traditional food and conversation. But, unlike my family, his family seemed incredibly loving and supportive.

As I looked around the family gathering, it wasn't long before my gaydar started going off. I told Arnel, "You never told me your brother[2] was gay."

"No, he's not gay," he protested.

I looked at him and said, "How many straight men do you know who sing gay classics like ABBA's *Dancing Queen* at their family's karaoke?"

He rolled his eyes as if to say, "Paul, you and your assumptions that everyone is gay." We've had that conversation before.

"And your brother's roommate of NINE years...pleee-aaasse," I muttered before reaching for more lumpia.

I felt at ease meeting his family but had more tea to spill after using the bathroom inside his aunt's small home.

"You didn't tell me your aunts[3] were a lesbian couple."

"What?! No...they are my favorite aunts[4]," he protested.

"Favorite aunts can be lesbians too."

"How do you know this?"

"One bedroom, one bed...one shared bed...do the math. And you were worried about coming out to your family! Why?"

Poor guy. This was all new to him, and I had decades of perfecting my gaydar!

I had a steep learning curve during my first Thanksgiving with Arnel and his family. Dinner was mostly potluck, and you served yourself with heavy paper plates from the dining room table. People were scattered throughout the house eating. There were traditions, like taking a group photo, and karaoke was always a family favorite. We have shared many family holidays since then, and I have grown to honor and embrace these traditions. Arnel's family became my *new* family. Our small circle of friends is my chosen family. They are an integral part of my happiness.

While my relationship with Arnel and his family was thriving, new discoveries emerged. After attending local storytelling events, I became mesmerized by these stories. I felt like each storyteller gave a gift of their soul. I reflected on their stories long after I heard them. I identified with these stories on a practical level. After over two decades in public service, I realized one of my gifts was sharing stories of how people benefited from our community programs. I now felt the need to tell my personal truths through storytelling.

While attending a work conference in Louisville, I discovered there was a Moth[5] storytelling event the last evening I was in town. I was determined to tell a story for the first time. I figured if I got called up, I would do my best. It's not like I knew anyone there anyway.

Local Moth storytelling productions are generally held in large bars with plenty of alcohol. The producers randomly select three sets of audience members as judges who then hold up their scores with large, laminated numbers: 9.2, 8.9, 9.4! The scores are tallied, and the performer with the highest total score is the winner. It's like the Olympics but with booze. Each event has an assigned topic, and each storyteller goes up on stage without notes or props. Oh, and there's a strict time limit. If you go over, the judges deduct points. Plus, every person who wants to perform puts their name in a hat and is randomly selected. So, you have no idea if you will even be called and, if you are, when you will be on stage. Nothing like all these rules to make this as nerve-wracking as possible.

To my amazement, I was called on stage. I really connected with the audience, and I placed second. That moment crystallized my desire to use my authentic voice to tell more stories. I was elated and excited to return to Portland and perform on stage. Storytelling at these Moth events gave me the courage to speak my truths, many for the first time. After a few years, I was ready to unshackle the "golden handcuffs" of my longtime job and the security it afforded me. I decided to work independently.

A few months into my career transition, hate speech and crimes were escalating at an alarming pace due to the 2016 presidential campaign. Much of this was fueled by Donald Trump's presidential campaign that was filled with acts of hatred and violence. In June, there was a mass shooting at Pulse, a gay bar in Orlando, Florida. This deadly, targeted crime was a major wake-up call to me and millions of others. When Trump was ultimately elected, I was despondent for most of November. I recall having to present an uplifting talk to a group of older adults. I tried getting out of doing it. The organizer said, "Paul, they need your light." I went ahead and did the event after her pep talk. I wasn't the only one who felt this way. Many friends were going through a similar form of depression and hopelessness.

The following year, I formed a storytelling company, Our Bold Voices, dedicated to amplifying marginalized voices. It was an extremely powerful experience, and our work continues today. When the Black Lives Matter movement became front and center, I reached out to storytellers I had mentored. Together we created new programming. With Arnel's help, we created these programs as webinars because it was during the early days of COVID. We continued to morph our storytelling presence from in person to online. I finally got to immerse myself in meaningful community work while being true to myself and others.

It was during this period of transformation, in my 50s, when I was called a "mensch" for the first time. I had to look it up to make sure I understood the meaning of the Yiddish term:

Mensch: A person of integrity and honor.

I was touched and honored. As I entered elderhood, I felt more comfortable hearing the word: Mensch. I have also discovered other realizations about myself:

Old nicknames no longer define me.

My family of choice functions like a well-adjusted biological family.

While I never experienced the playfulness of being a Zoom kid, I experience a different kind of freedom as an elder ON Zoom.

Abnormal. Pathological. Deviant. Sick...

Those words were replaced years ago. Survivor. Resilient. Mensch.

Endnotes

1 Unitarian Universalism, or UU, is a liberal religious body encouraging spiritual growth. While historically Christian, the Unitarian Universalist church does not adhere to religious creed. Instead, its members commit to seven principles, beginning with a belief in "the inherent worth and dignity of every person." This inclusive religious community has a longstanding tradition of being LGBTQ+ welcoming.

2 His brother and boyfriend came out to the family a few years later. They also married after we did.

3 The term aunt or auntie in some cultures extend beyond traditional biological or legal parameters. In Arnel's eyes, these unmarried aunts provided loving support and no distinction was ever made regarding blood lines while growing up. That continues today.

4 They are my favorite aunts too! I have a unique relationship with each of them.

5 Founded in 1997, The Moth has many different formats that focus around live storytelling. Here, I'm referencing the beginning stage of their live community events, also known as StorySLAMS, where everyday people with a desire to share their story had a chance of getting up on stage. "Winners" from those events could gain more experience and exposure by competing in GrandSLAMS where the same rules apply but are held in larger venues.

Author's Note

Part of my journey has been reconciling and forgiving those who contributed to making me feel like a misfit. Time and distance have created a convenient buffer—sometimes.

While I was wrapping up this story, I visited my 92-year-old dad back in the East Coast. After a series of health setbacks, he recently moved into an assisted living community. I felt like it was time for a visit, and without much notice, Arnel and I were on a plane.

My phone conversations with my dad had always been surface, superficial, and without much depth. I wondered if this visit would be different. Would he open up more about his feelings and not just complain about the food there? Did he have a desire to deepen our disconnected bond? Would he tell me he was proud of me?

My father sat by the front door of the sunny facility entryway like an old, treasured pet, dozing while waiting for his family's return. Word about our visit had already spread fast, despite just calling him the night before to arrange a time. Residents and staff were waiting for our arrival. My dad never remembers my hubby's name but introduced Arnel as "my friend." When I had the opportunity to introduce myself to anyone, I said, "It's good to meet you. My name is Paul. I am Frankie's son. and this is my husband, Arnel."

I didn't realize it at the time, but my dad took notice. Later on that day, when introducing me, he made sure to say, "and this is his husband." It warmed my heart each time he said it, casually and with ease. Did I detect a hint of pride? Maybe.

Our visit helped my dad's street cred with his peers and the staff. It was their version of the day's headline story: "New Resident's Son from West Coast Visits Father." Apparently, this was big news, especially since our trip wasn't the result of him having a health emergency or cramming this visit in during a business trip.

I struggled with managing expectations of myself and others. Our relationship has been a series of awkward and confusing missteps for most of my life. The same goes for my five siblings. When our mom died some 30 years ago, there was no longer an incentive to stay connected. She was the crazy glue that held our fractured family together.

That's not the version that's expressed to the outside world. You are Italians. Of course your family is close. That's simply not the case. Years of mistrust, abuse, manipulation, perfectionism, intimidation, and untreated mental illness have created an unresolvable void between us.

This visit brought up stored memories that I protectively packed away decades ago. I was caught off guard and needed time and space to process these feelings.

On my last day there, we picked up a large pizza and shared it with my dad in the common area. My dad loves being the center of attention, and I was glad we could elevate his profile and social standing in his new communal setting.

Prior to leaving, my dad—the ultimate prankster—started throwing his voice. He did this when I was a kid but I forgot until now. He said, "Let me outta here." A few staff and residents looked bewildered. I glanced over at my dad. He had that knowing smile on his face. That look of self-satisfaction that expressed, "I may be old, but I've still got it!"

When I reflect on that recent visit, there's really nothing earth-shattering to unpack. Just the reality that we have never been close, and we can't recreate something that never existed. Instead, I try to remember us eating pizza together and the lightness and playfulness of that moment.

I guess that's all part of being a mensch!

Paul (he/him) credits his upbringing in a large, Italian, East Coast family for helping him speak up at the dining room table, lest he go unheard. Having lived in Portland, Oregon, for over 30 years, he enjoys performing, producing shows, creating documentaries, teaching, and coaching. Paul is known nationally for his contributions to the field of LGBTQ+ aging. This is Paul's second anthology, after the publication of COVIDOLOGY (www.ourboldvoices.com/covidology) in 2022. He's excited about the opportunities for Defining Moments *to reflect our true history and amplify LGBTQ+ voices. You can follow Paul at* www.ourboldvoices.com.

Misfit to Mensch

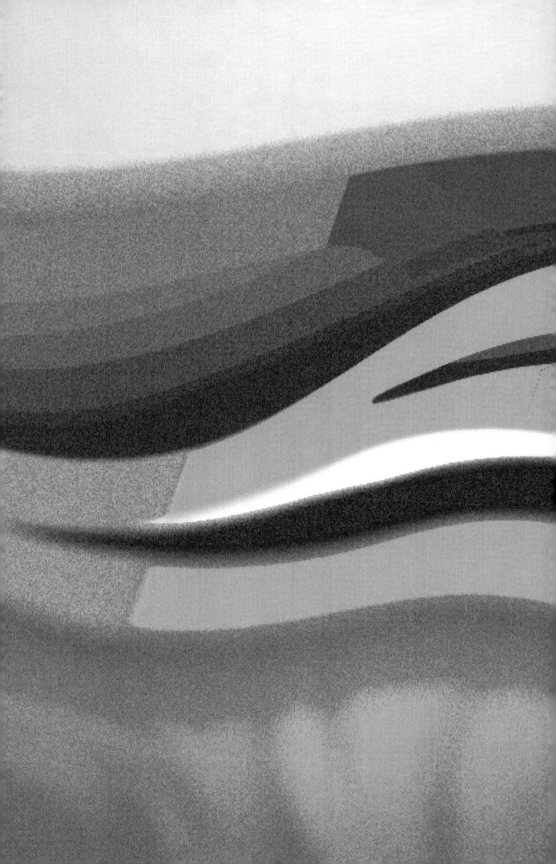

Set Free

By Stacey Rice

The large glass entrance doors to Duke University Medical's endocrinology clinic were right in front of me, but I couldn't move. The rhythmic swinging of the doors as people came and went hypnotically captured me as I pondered the unknowns waiting for me. My new life was just beyond those swinging doors, but my nerves stopped me for the moment.

It had taken a lot to get me to this place. The past 37 years of my life were consumed with the knowledge I was transgender. Those long years held many things including a desperate search for a remedy that would lift this burden.

It was why I was standing in front of these doors. I was here to see an endocrinologist who could prescribe the miracle drugs that would set me free.

With an invisible nudge from the universe, I finally stepped across the threshold and into a packed waiting room. I found a chair wedged in a corner and it became progressively harder for me to sit there as the minutes clicked by. Was it the chair or my nerves that caused me to squirm?

My name was eventually called, and I followed the nurse down a labyrinth of sterile hallways lined with randomly-placed oak doors. Our steps made no sound as we made our way along the highly polished vinyl floor. She continued to quietly lead me until we came to one of the last doors and into a treatment room. She took my blood pressure and heart rate, and both reflected my sky-high feelings at that moment. She told me the doctor would be right in. Taking one quick glance at me, she walked out and closed the door.

I sat there counting down the seconds until I could finally begin my new life. My head was filled with a swirling collection of thoughts. I was anxious about what would happen next. I was lucky to find this doctor since this type of information was hard to come by in 1999. I asked my trans friends whom I should go see, and they gave me his name. They told me he was an accepting person—but was he really?

From a dark corner of my mind, I wondered whether I would have to prove I was transgender. That thought prompted me to compose a mental checklist of all the reasons why I knew I was. At the top of the list was the deep knowing that I was female inside this male body. That knowledge had not budged since I was 5 years old. I kept going over and over my list until there was a knock at the door and it opened.

A tall middle-aged man in a white lab coat with a floppy stethoscope tied around his neck stepped in and introduced himself. He asked why I was here and in a very tentative voice, I replied, "I am transgender, and I want to start hormone therapy." He asked, "Do you have a letter of support from a mental health provider?"

I was ready for that question. I knew that a doctor treating transgender patients would likely be using the standards of care issued by the World Professional Association for Transgender Health[1]. As part of those standards, an evaluation and letter of support by a licensed mental health provider was needed before treatment could begin.

I gave him my letter, and after taking time to read it, he shared the details of what the beginning of my new life would look like. His words washed over me like a pure stream of spring water, quenching a thirst that had built up in me for decades. My journey would start with a hefty daily dose of estrogen and a testosterone blocker, which would help the estrogen take effect. That would continue for the rest of my life.

There were side effects to be considered. He started down a list of the more serious ones that might come with taking estrogen—depression, memory loss, and blood clots that could lead to a heart attack or stroke. This seemed like a small price to pay to free myself from the burden that had weighed on me for decades.

When all my questions were answered, he reached into his lab coat pocket and pulled out a prescription pad. As he wrote the prescription for the drugs that would change my life, I felt the personal hell of the last 37 years slowly being erased with each stroke of his pen.

I was in a daze as I walked back along the vinyl floor and into the busy waiting room. Patients, nurses, and doctors floated by me as I found my way back through the glass doors and over the threshold into my new life. My emotions hit with the force of a tornado—joy, fear, adrenaline, anxiety—they all arose in the five minutes it took me to walk to my car. I sat down in the driver's seat and released a long breath—almost a subconscious breath—one that I had been holding tightly for years. As I exhaled, the invisible weight, which had crushed my soul for so long, took wing on every molecule of breath that I pushed out. I was finally released.

Each day I faithfully took my miracle drugs. The physical changes I experienced were many—softer skin, fat redistribution, breast growth. My eyes and face developed a more feminine appearance. As I noticed the changes occurring in me, it was like watching a miracle manifest right in front of my eyes. A joyful miracle resulting from my body changing with each milligram of estrogen and testosterone blocker that was slowly being released.

With my facial features softening, I never knew how people would address me when I left my apartment. I dressed pretty androgynously as I hadn't yet fully transitioned to living as my female self. Every trip out was a gender adventure. I constantly felt like I was participating in a game of "spinning pronoun" roulette with each and every interaction.

I was in Walgreens the first time it happened. As I wandered down the aisle, an employee walked up and said, "Ma'am is there anything I can help you with?" For a split second, I was lost for words as I had never been addressed this way. I stammered back in my best female voice, "No, I am doing fine." As I continued down the aisle, I said to myself, "Oh my god, I got my first ma'am!" But then as I walked out of the Walgreens and into the Harris Teeter grocery store next door, a man almost ran into me, and he jumped back saying, "Oh sorry, sir." From joy to disappointment in under 30 seconds. Even though it was for a short time, I did realize that "ma'am" fit me just fine.

I needed to get my name changed. My parents gave me the name Stuart when I was born—after my father. I started trying out different female names to see which one would fit. I ran them by my friend Lauren. As we sat having dinner one night, I shared my latest list with her. She became exasperated and said, "All of these are awful. To me, you feel like what a woman named Stacey would be like. So, you are Stacey!" And she was right. It wasn't long before I received a document that said in bold letters: "It is hereby ordered that the name of the party be changed to Stacey Anne Rice."

The final piece of my transition was getting a new driver's license with my female face and new name joyfully splashed across the front of it. I didn't quite know what to expect at the Department of Motor Vehicles (DMV) office, which was just down the street from my apartment. I got dressed as Stacey, and as I sat in the parking lot of the office, I kept repeating over and over again, "Universe, please don't let there be many people in there." And almost at the same time, "Please make sure the DMV employees are nice and not stern and judgmental." I continued my mantra as I got out of the car and made my way to the waiting room.

As I sat there, I focused on each and every employee, desperately trying to ascertain which one would be the most accepting. Soon, my number was called by the lone female employee in the office. As I sat down at her desk, she asked me what I needed. With my throat so incredibly dry, I croaked out, "I just had my name changed, and I need to get a new license." She took my existing license and my name change document and intently stared at it for a minute or two. As I sat there silently, my mind was racing trying to guess what her next words would be.

She finally looked up, pointed down at my license and said, "You want to change this don't you?" I glanced down briefly with confusion as I thought she was pointing towards my name. I didn't understand her because I had just given her my name change document. I answered, "My name?"

She said, "No, this." She was pointing at the gender marker on my license—the" M" that had been there since I was 16 years old.

Now I was even more confused. In North Carolina at that time, trans people couldn't change the sex assigned to us at birth on any of our legal documents unless we had gender-confirming surgery. If so, the surgeon who had done the surgery had to certify in writing they had performed the appropriate clinical treatment for a person's new gender[2].

It was incredibly hard to find a surgeon who did gender-confirming surgery back then. There were only a small handful in the United States who performed this surgery. It was expensive, and no medical insurance carrier would cover it. There were stipulations in each carrier's medical insurance policy under the Exceptions to Coverage section that explicitly stated that no coverage would be extended to any treatment for "transsexualism and/or sex-change surgery," as it was worded back then[3].

As a result of this and for other reasons, I had not gone through surgery. I had resigned myself to having the "M" on my new license. But it slowly dawned on me that she was pointing to the gender marker. I said with a quivering conviction, "I thought that couldn't be changed unless I had surgery?" She looked up at me, glanced around at her co-workers, and quietly said, "Honey, you are not the first one to come in here. Wouldn't you want this changed?" I almost shouted as I replied, "Yes, I would." And she did.

I started living full-time as my female self not too long after the DMV visit. I found my first job as Stacey. However, I had to start my work career over since transitioning. Acceptance at my previous job was not possible. I struggled financially for some time after transitioning. It was hard making ends meet working at Dillard's department store for $10 an hour—ironically as a sales associate in the men's department. But no matter how hard those struggles were, my life overflowed every day with a joy that permeated my heart and soul. A joy that came from listening to my heart and becoming who I was always meant to be—a trans woman whose soul had finally been set free.

Endnotes

1 The World Professional Association for Transgender Health, formerly the Harry Benjamin International Gender Dysphoria Association, first published a "Standard of Care for the Health of Transgender and Gender Diverse People" in 1979. It was developed to provide clinical guidance and education to health professionals who assist transgender people. The Standard of Care has been updated several times over the years and is still the main resource for health professionals.

2 Twenty years after my experience at the North Carolina DMV in 1999, the Department released a new "sex designation form" making it easier for transgender people to have the proper gender on their N.C. driver's licenses. The

form only requires a medical or mental health professional to attest that "in my professional opinion, the applicant's gender identity is male or female." There is not an option to attest to for people who identify as gender non-binary.

3 Starting in 2014, the Federal Affordable Care Act prohibited insurers from discriminating on the basis of gender or gender identification. It was made illegal for private insurance plans to deny coverage for medically necessary transition-related care. Unfortunately, in 2023, over 100 bills were introduced in state legislatures that would ban gender-affirming medical care. Most of these bills prohibit gender-affirming care for people under 18 years of age, but some states have introduced measures that would extend to adults as well.

Stacey (she/her) is a speaker, educator, consultant, and community leader on transgender issues. She has been recognized as a Queer Hero by the Gay & Lesbian Archives of the Pacific NW and is the former Executive Co-Director of Portland's Q Center. She is one of the stars of the documentary, Who's on Top? LGBTQs Summit Mt. Hood (nosunrisewasted.com/whosontop). The documentary profiles the lives of four LGBTQ+ community members and how they overcame the obstacles that stood like mountains in their lives. She is also a recipient of a 2023 Oregon Humanities Community Storytelling Fellowship. You can find her at www.staceyrice.com.

My Struggle for Acceptance

By James W. Sutherland

knew I was "different" when I entered first grade in 1948. Remember the game Spin the Bottle? Once, when the spinning bottle stopped in front of me, my friends told me I could kiss anyone I wanted. So, I kissed the boy sitting next to me because I thought he was cute. I was never invited back to play Spin the Bottle with them again.

During recess I joined the girls for hopscotch and jump rope. I was much better at those games than I ever was at kickball and dodgeball. Later, when all the boys I knew were talking about wanting to kiss the girls, I wondered, "Why?"

When I was 6, my parents divorced, and I moved around a lot. Many of the moves happened in the middle of a school year. I was almost always the new kid at school. By age 10, I had attended six different grade schools. They became a refuge during the upheavals in my young life.

All my teachers were older women who gifted me with a sense of self-worth by listening to me and providing encouragement. They seemed to know I lacked emotional support at home. Whatever the reason, they were always kind to me.

All except Miss Mapleton.

It was 1951. I was living with my father in a low-rent neighborhood in Denver. I was in third grade and the new kid at yet another school. This time my transfer happened a month before the end of the school year. Making friends as a newcomer in any school was never easy for me. School would soon be out, so I didn't even try this time.

The school had an in-house library. Once a week, my third-grade class went to a large room where we sat and read for one hour. Miss Mapleton was the librarian. Long before I was born, she had established a set of regulations for what she called "proper behavior." Once we crossed the threshold into *her* library, we were expected to follow every one of *her* rules.

On library day, Miss Mapleton stood guard at the entrance door watching as we third graders walked in and took our seats at one of many library tables. We sat in silence with our hands folded. No one moved until Miss Mapleton announced, *"All right children, you may retrieve your books. And remember, NO STOPPING. NO TALKING. AND ONLY ONE WAY TRAFFIC IN THE LIBRARY."*

At her signal, we all rose and in single file, like little storm troopers, marched over to one special wall of books. As we walked by the books, each child reached out without stopping, grabbed a book, and returned to their seat to read.

This was my first time in the library. I was already anxious about the librarian's intimidating demeanor. My classmates all knew exactly which book they wanted, but I had no idea which book I should take.

Miss Mapleton offered me no help and then I made my first mistake. I stopped. How else could I decide which book I wanted to read? As the kids bumped into me, I apologized with, "I'm sorry." My second mistake: I spoke. Glaring at me, Miss Mapleton reminded us in a loud voice, *"NO STOPPING. NO TALKING. ONLY ONE WAY TRAFFIC IN THE LIBRARY."*

I was confused and beginning to not like Miss Mapleton. Scared and self-conscious, I turned the wrong way. I walked back toward Miss Mapleton. My third mistake. She now glared directly at me and screamed, *"ONLY ONE WAY TRAFFIC IN THE LIBRARY."*

Like a little automaton, I instantly turned in my tracks. As fast as I could, I walked away from Miss Mapleton, unsure what to do next. Since I was the only kid in the room without a book, she snarled at me to start over. Under the critical eye of Miss Mapleton, I made another attempt. By now I was certain she had labeled me a troublemaker for violating all three of her rules. This time around, knowing I was not allowed to stop and take time to look, I decided to grab a book. Any book. I didn't care which book. The bright orange spine of a book caught my eye, so I snatched it and hurried back to my seat at the table.

I looked to see what book I grabbed. It turned out to be *Louisa May Alcott, Girl of Old Boston*[1]. As I started reading, I was mesmerized. The characters were living in a different time when there were no cars or radios. They traveled in beautiful coaches like Cinderella, and the girls wore long dresses. Louisa May Alcott's family lived in a beautiful house. She slept in a frilly, four-poster, canopied bed. When I saw a picture of her bed, I was sure I would like to have one, too.

All was well until Miss Mapleton, on patrol, came up to my seat and looked over my shoulder to see what I was reading. You can imagine my 8-year-old shock when she grabbed the book out of my hands and announced to the entire room, *"Louisa May Alcott is not the kind of book any boy should be reading."* The kids roared with laughter. As the new kid, I slunk down in my seat, embarrassed and humiliated.

Miss Mapleton then turned and marched over to the wall of books. She seized a different one, brought it back, and dropped it like a rock in front of me. *"This is the kind of book boys should read,"* she bellowed. It was *Daniel Boone, Boy Hunter of Old Kentucky.*

I reluctantly turned the pages. Daniel Boone carried a rifle, hunted, killed bears, and was always on the lookout for "savages." Apparently, there were no beautiful carriages in Kentucky because he walked everywhere. He lived in an ugly log cabin, and I suspected Daniel Boone didn't sleep in a frilly, four-poster, canopied bed. I hated Daniel Boone. I hated Miss Mapleton even more for taking Louisa May Alcott away from me before I could finish reading her story.

Then school was out for the summer. My father and I moved yet again. While I was finally free of Miss Mapleton's library, the shadow of my experience there never left me. And I never forgot Louisa May Alcott either.

That September, right before I became the new kid in fourth grade at a different school, my father took me shopping for school clothes. Because he didn't make a lot of money, we went to Goodwill, a place I thought everyone shopped.

While in the book section, a bright orange spine jumped out at me. I was dumbfounded. On the shelf sat a copy of *Louisa May Alcott, Girl of Old Boston* on sale for 20 cents.

I ran to my father and begged for two dimes so I could rescue my lost book friend off the shelf. I took the slim orange volume home, and I finished reading about Louisa May Alcott. I had defied Miss Mapleton's warning that it was not a book for boys. Although she did not witness my rebellious act, the moment was empowering to this 8-year-old. To celebrate my small victory, I took a green crayon and wrote on the inside cover in my best third grade handwriting, *"This book belongs to James Sutherland."*

I did not forget Miss Mapleton and her repressive pronouncements. The humiliation I felt that day stayed with me. Long after third grade, I wondered why she took a book I wanted to read away from me and why boys shouldn't read it.

Miss Mapleton's public shaming of me in front of my classmates had an immediate effect. I wondered if there was something wrong with me. My third grader's heart said, *"No."* But because of her harsh judgment, I felt threatened. I wanted to hide. Unconsciously, I began laying the foundation of a closet I would later hide in.

Over the years I would encounter other Miss Mapletons, ready to remind me I didn't fit in. I didn't understand when I heard judgmental parents say, *"Jack and Suzie can't play with you anymore."*

The taunts from other boys my age hurt even more. *"You're a sissy. You throw the ball like a girl. You better watch out. No one likes you. Go away."*

It was on the playground that I first heard the word "queer[2]." I was in eighth grade. It was a crude and hateful curse reserved to bash those, like myself, who were different. I wasn't sure what queer meant, but I knew it was bad.

It was also on the playground when I heard kids talk about a boy whose parents had him locked up in a mental hospital[3] when they found out he was queer. Whether or not this really happened didn't matter. I became even more fearful, and the story haunted me. I worried my parents might do the same if they thought I was queer.

When I turned 14, I started high school. I was terrified of what any of the boys would do to me if they found out just how different I really was. My closet, under construction since third grade, was ready for my occupancy, and I moved right in.

Despite my fears, high school was not the catastrophe I anticipated. One of my best grade school friends was a neighbor girl. She was outgoing, kind, smart, and beautiful. Rosalie was popular and was elected freshman cheerleader. All the boys in football had a crush on her. While the jocks may have thought about harassing me, none of them dared because I was Rosalie's close friend.

Still, I worked hard to keep classmates away from my closet. I learned early on that most people love to talk about themselves. So, when the curious asked me dangerous personal questions, I diverted the conversation by asking them questions. I also used my sense of humor. Getting my classmates to laugh was a reliable way to distract them.

I once overheard my stepmother explain to a nosy neighbor why I didn't date. She said I was too busy studying to have time for girls. I quickly, and eagerly, adopted that role. Sadly, even though I had lots of friends including many girls, none of them really knew me. I had been successful at keeping everyone at a safe distance for four years as I continued to occupy my closet.

In the fall of 1960, I started college. In grade school, I had been more curious about the boys than the girls. Now, on campus, I started noticing men. Some of the looks I received in return lingered in a way that made me uncomfortable. Despite my raging hormones, I was too naïve, too closeted to understand why. Did they wonder if I was queer?

Inspired by my grade school instructors, who had played a significant role in my childhood, I wanted to become a teacher. Unfortunately, my ambition was thwarted at the beginning of my third year. A counselor advised me to consider another profession. When I asked why, he said, *"A man like you would never be hired to instruct children."* When I persisted, he could not (or would not) elaborate on what he had said.

But his implication was clear. *"Like you,"* meant something was wrong with me. The humiliation I felt in Miss Mapleton's library returned. So did my old question, "What was wrong with what I felt in my heart?" The 8-year-old me had been confused. But the 21-year-old me was angry. I dropped out of college at the end of that semester.

In 1963 there was no legal recourse for me, or any gay person, to confront such blatant discrimination. My only choice was to move on. Leaving college created inevitable questions from my family and friends. *"Why did you drop out? I thought you wanted to become a teacher. What happened?"*

The severe consequences of telling the truth kept me from even considering it. I lied, *"I need a break for a while. Don't worry. I'm going back."* Still trapped in my closet, I felt more alone than ever. The walls began to push in on me.

I thought about going away to a place where no one knew me. Then maybe I'd figure things out myself. I studied maps to see just how far away from Denver I could get with the money I had saved.

One of my other grade school "girlfriends," Iris, returned to Denver from the West Coast where she had moved after high school. Although I wanted to, I could not explain to her why I had dropped out. But Iris suspected.

She said *"Jim, maybe you need to do what I did. Get the hell out of Denver. Maybe go to California. I think you might like it out there."* Iris probably knew I was gay before I did.

Iris' advice kept tugging at me, so I headed for the West Coast. But California wasn't far enough away. I only stayed long enough to board a freighter bound for Honolulu. We sailed from San Francisco on November 19, 1963. Four days later, while still at sea, we received the shocking news President Kennedy had been assassinated.

As soon as the ship docked, I headed for Waikiki Beach. It was a joyous feeling to be anonymous. I lost myself in the throngs of tourists, sailors, and the airline and ship crews swarming the streets of Waikiki. I was more relaxed than I had ever been in my entire life.

I saw vast numbers of people coming and going. The mix of races and nationalities living there was a life-altering experience for this 21-year-old who had never traveled far from Colorado.

Jobs were plentiful. In no time, I was working as a room service waiter in a large hotel. Within a month, I rented a studio apartment one block off Waikiki Beach for $100 a month.

Hawaii's "live and let live" attitude was irresistible. I discovered many gay men living in Waikiki including some of my coworkers at the hotel. We all knew who we were, but most were like me. We weren't completely out of the closet.

We met and socialized in our own underground community where I was welcomed and supported. I finally fit in. I had never been happier. I wasn't completely out in Hawaii, but I was much closer to the closet door.

One morning at work, Daniel, one of the waiters, pulled me aside to ask if I had heard about a fight the night before at The Clouds, a gay bar a block from where I lived. When I said, *"No,"* he couldn't wait to share details.

A friend of his, who was a witness, said two muscle-bound Polynesian men, both over six feet, came into the bar. The manager told them to leave. When I asked why, Daniel's answer stunned me.

"Because both were wearing dresses. And high heels. And make-up." If he had said they were Martians, it would have been more believable.

According to the friend, the pair left, then returned later with four other tall, muscular Polynesian men, also wearing dresses, high heels, and make-up. The six angry men burst into the bar and started throwing chairs, up-ending tables, and smashing everything in sight. Terrified customers ran for the door.

The manager called the police. After surveying the scene, the cops backed away and stood idly by as the men continued to demolish the bar. When their work was done, they calmly walked past the police, out the door, and disappeared into the night.

Daniel's friend said the police did not intervene because they were familiar with some of the men. None of the cops thought it was worth getting injured by trying to subdue them over some beef they had with the bar.

I wasn't sure if the bizarre story was true, so I walked by The Clouds on the way home from work. Seeing the smashed entrance door and boarded up windows ended my skepticism. The bar remained closed for weeks.

I scoured every inch of news in *The Honolulu Advertiser* for days afterward looking for a story about the incident. I never found one.

In the spring of 1965, a coworker moved to San Francisco. Soon after, I received a letter describing his adventures in the Big City. One line captured my attention: *"Jim, you've got to move here. There are no closets in San Francisco."*

In 1966, I arrived in San Francisco on my 24th birthday. The walls of my closet gave way, the door opened, and the heavy weight I had carried since grade school started slipping away.

San Francisco represented a freedom I never expected to have in my lifetime. My days of living underground were over. I no longer had to deny the truth about myself just to stay safe.

I found thousands of gay men and women in my new home who were living "normal" lives. I realized I had the same opportunity. I finally stopped being afraid.

While the city seemed like the end of the rainbow, it was not perfect.

The first job I applied for was with the telephone company. I was told after my interview, *"We do not hire your kind."* I was surprised. My gut screamed, *"What? That guy behind the desk is gayer than you are."*

Despite my disappointment, there was no legal way to challenge such discrimination at that time, not even in San Francisco.

In the mid-60s, police raids on gay bars were routine. In response, the bar owners formed the Tavern Guild[4] in 1962.

It would take a few years, and more bar owners joining the organization, before Tavern Guild had the power to push back at City Hall. But when they did, the police raids on the gay bars stopped.

The summer I arrived, a riot erupted at Compton's Cafeteria[5], an all-night eatery in the Tenderloin[6]. Drag queens were harassed, beaten, and arrested in a vicious police response. The cafeteria was trashed.

News of the riots swept through the gay community. The next morning I went with a couple of friends to take a look at the damage. Compton's was closed and the broken windows boarded up.

Although out, I was still naïve about many facets of gay life. However, while standing on the glass-strewn sidewalk, I got a crash course on "the world of drag" from my two older and wiser companions.

It was then that memories of the story Daniel told me in Waikiki returned. Now I understood who the "men in dresses" were and why they had destroyed The Clouds bar in a rampage.

Like the Compton rioters, those six men had also suffered ridicule and discrimination because of their cross-dressing. The distance between the bar and the cafeteria

was 3,000 miles. Yet in the space of a few years, both locations witnessed similar explosions of suppressed rage.
Oppressed minorities in both places, with nothing to lose,
chose to openly fight for rights they had been denied. It was
just the beginning.

In 1967, during the "Summer of Love," my gay friends
and I grew beards and long hair. We went to free concerts in
Golden Gate Park and protested the Vietnam War. We also
experimented with grass and dropped acid (LSD).

During the early 1970s, I saw dramatic changes in the
Castro area as more gay men and lesbians arrived seeking
the same refuge I had. This migration brought energy to the
birth of the Gay Liberation Movement.

As newcomers became politically active, it was Harvey Milk who understood their potential power if they organized into a larger group.

In 1977, after two failed attempts, he was elected to
the Board of Supervisors. He reached a pinnacle no other gay
man or lesbian had ever attained in San Francisco. He had
broken through the Lavender Ceiling.

I went to City Hall with two friends to witness Har-
vey's swearing in by Dianne Feinstein[7], President of the
Board of Supervisors. I was overcome with a sense of pride.
We finally had a trusted voice in City Hall to represent us.
We had Harvey, and I had a right to be in that building. I'd
never felt that way before Harvey's election.

Our joy was short-lived. On November 27, 1978, an assassin's bullet ended both the lives of Mayor George Moscone[8] and Harvey Milk. Their untimely deaths were a gut punch to the entire community.

By early evening, word of the assassination spread and people by the thousands poured into the streets, all headed for the intersection of Market and Castro. I joined five of my friends as the masses began a spontaneous march toward City Hall[9].

Silence overwhelmed the crowd. No one spoke. The only sounds I heard were weeping and soft footsteps as we walked in cadence to the slow beating of drums in the crowd. A phalanx of lighted candles surrounded me.

A block away from Civic Center, I heard a familiar voice singing *Amazing Grace*. My suspicions were confirmed when we reached City Hall. Joan Baez was at the microphone.

Six months later, the jury verdict[10] was announced on the five o'clock news. Dan White[11], who shot and killed Harvey Milk and Mayor Moscone, was convicted of involuntary manslaughter and received only an eight-year prison sentence for both murders. A shock wave rippled through the entire city.

Once again with friends, I joined throngs gathering at Market and Castro. This time, we weren't there for a mournful walk. Rage about the verdict fueled the crowd. We jammed onto the trolleys and buses bound for Civic Center.

When we reached City Hall, a riot was in full swing. I saw men pulling parking meters out of the cement sidewalk with their bare hands. These became projectiles hurled through the windows, followed by trash cans and newspaper stands that had been set afire. The crowd was intent on burning City Hall down.

I was never a violent person. But that night my suppressed anger sprang up and turned into a bolt of fury that exploded inside of me. It was born out of regret for my wasted years hiding in the closet; opportunities lost because of the discrimination I encountered.

I joined the mob of other angry gay men, screaming and throwing whatever I could find. I ignored those who pleaded with all of us to stop and to go home.

Later, the crowd advanced on 11 parked police cars and started smashing windshields. One by one, each car was torched. I broke down crying when I saw the flames and the smoke, followed by the sounds of sirens going off one after another.

My vengeance was finally spent. All I could think of was the damage done to my beautiful city, the place that had given me the freedom to be who I really was.

I felt despondent that all that Harvey had achieved for us seemed lost with his death. And what remained was now destroyed by the riot.

Even though the violence continued that night, I wanted to go home. My friends and I walked in silence up Market Street to the Castro. Lost in my thoughts, I kept wondering over and over, *"How is our community ever going to recover?"* I had no answer[12].

I never forgot Miss Mapleton's admonishment in her library nor understood the reasons for her motivation. As a child, I thought she was just mean. As an adult I realize that, whatever her reason, what she said turned out to be a prophetic warning about the difficulties ahead for a boy like me who was "different."

It was also my first experience defying censorship. I read *Louisa May Alcott, Girl of Old Boston* anyway. The most valuable lesson to come out of our encounter, but probably not the one Miss Mapleton intended, was that I learned to trust my heart about what was right for me.

I still have my copy of *Louisa May Alcott, Girl of Old Boston*; the one I bought as a child at the Goodwill. It has always had a place in my bookcase wherever I've lived.

Like its owner, its once bright cover has faded. Stress marks and other signs of aging are visible on both of us. Not surprising. The small volume is just a year younger than I am. It was printed in 1943.

Endnotes

1 Louisa May Alcott was a nineteenth century American novelist, poet, and short story writer. She is best known for her classics *Little Women* (1868), *Little Men* (1871), and *Jo's Boys* (1886).

2 In my youth, "queer" was a vicious and hurtful word. I recall ACT-UP (AIDS Coalition to Unleash Power), a grassroots organization and their in-your-face demonstrations in the late 1980s. Demonstrators flipped the word "queer" on its head by embracing it as a badge of honor instead of a weapon used against us. It's taken decades for me to hear the word without cringing. The first time I remember owning the word "queer" was at a pride parade in the 1990s when I heard the now familiar chant, "We're here. We're queer. Get used to it."

3 During the 1940s and 1950s, the American Psychiatric Association (APA) classified homosexuality as a "mental disorder." Accepted medical "conversion therapy" at that time included drugs, electric shock, and lobotomies. Minors under the age of 18 suspected of being homosexual could be legally committed by their parents to a mental hospital for compulsory "treatment." It would take another 20 years of scientific research and studies on homosexuality before the APA declassified homosexuality as a mental disorder in 1973.

4 The Tavern Guild was formed in 1962 by San Francisco gay bar owners in response to random and continuous police raids on their bars. Members met regularly to orga-

nize against the systematic discrimination they collectively faced. They set up a "telephone tree" network to alert each other of raids. They eventually grew stronger and confronted City Hall about San Francisco Police Department's targeted and discriminatory practices. As a united front, they also challenged discrimination by state agencies like the California Department of Alcoholic Beverage Control. Within a few years, the police harassment and random raids on gay bars stopped.

5 Compton's Cafeteria was an all-night restaurant and a popular gathering spot for drag queens and trans people, particularly trans women, seeking a place to hang out after the bars closed at 2 a.m. Compton's managers often called the police to remove drag queens and trans women from the cafeteria. In 1966, in San Francisco like many United States cities, it was against the law to dress as a person of the opposite sex. Police used the "female impersonation" law as an excuse to harass and arrest gender nonconforming people.

The Compton Cafeteria Riot began when a police officer tried to arrest a transgender woman. She threw her cup of coffee in his face and fighting erupted inside the restaurant and poured out into the streets. This riot preceded the Stonewall Riots by three years. The Stonewall Riots lasted for several days but Compton's was over in a few hours because rioters were quickly overpowered and hauled off to jail. The Compton Cafeteria Riot did not have the same effect nationally as Stonewall. But it was the beginning of City Hall acknowledging and ending police brutality towards transgender women. It was also the birth of transgender activism in San Francisco. Compton's Cafeteria's business declined after the riot and closed in 1972. Screaming Queens, an EMMY award winning documentary released in 2005, tells the little-known story of this historic 1966 collective act of resistance for civil rights.

6 The Tenderloin was considered the "unseemly" side of San Francisco. It was home to high crime, prostitution, drugs, gambling halls, gay bars, bathhouses, drag nightclubs, porn theaters, and all-night eateries, including Compton's Cafeteria. Low rents attracted an eclectic and colorful population including immigrants, elderly, and LGBTQ+ residents.

7 Dianne Feinstein was a politician known for her long tenure as a California State senator from 1992 until her death in 2023. She was elected to the San Francisco Board of Supervisors in 1969 and immediately became the board's first female president upon her appointment in 1970. During her third term as the board's president in 1978, Feinstein succeeded Moscone as mayor after the brutal assassinations of Mayor George Moscone and City Supervisor Harvey Milk. She became the first woman to serve as Mayor.

8 George Moscone was an attorney and Democratic politician and the 37th mayor of San Francisco from January 1976 until his assassination in November 1978. He was known as "The People's Mayor" because he believed in inclusion, He supported opening City Hall and its commissions to reflect the diversity of San Francisco's population.

9 An impromptu candlelight march started in the Castro leading to the City Hall steps. Tens of thousands

attended. The San Francisco Gay Men's Chorus sang Felix Mendelssohn's Thou, Lord our Refuge. It was their first-ever public performance. The crowd carried flowers and lit candles. So many candles were placed at the base of the Abraham Lincoln statue that it appeared to be ablaze from a distance.

A recorded speech Harvey gave three weeks earlier was played over the sound system. It was his response to the defeat of the California Briggs Initiative in a statewide election earlier in November. This anti-gay ballot sought to ban gays and lesbians from working in California public schools. In the recording, Harvey spoke about the importance of showing the rest of the country our strength through our numbers. He called for every gay person who was not out to come out. He also asked the crowd to try to understand the positions of people who were responsible for getting the Briggs Initiative on the ballot in the first place.

Two days after the assassination, the bodies of both men were brought to the City Hall Rotunda where thousands of mourners paid their respects.

10 Dan White's arrest and trial revealed the tensions between liberal and conservative communities as well as divisions between the gay community and the city police. His jury was made up mostly of White, middle-class San Franciscans. Gays and ethnic minorities were excluded from the jury pool.

The jury found White guilty of voluntary manslaughter rather than first-degree murder. He was sentenced to serve seven years in prison. Outrage within San Francisco's gay community over his sentencing sparked the city's White Night riots.

11 Dan White was elected as a Democrat to the San Francisco Board of Supervisors in 1972. He was convicted of manslaughter for the deaths of Milk and Moscone and served five years of a seven-year prison sentence. Less than two years after his release, he returned to San Francisco and later committed suicide in 1985.

12 The May 22 and May 23, 1979, editions of *The San Francisco Chronicle* and *The San Francisco Examiner* provided extensive coverage of these events. In summary:

Damages in Civic Center buildings, including City Hall, City Library, and several state office buildings, amounted to $1 million.

The estimated number of rioters was between 2,000 and 3,000. Sixty civilians were injured, 20 rioters were arrested, and 59 police officers were injured.

Dianne Feinstein and several supervisors were sequestered in City Hall during the riot.

Carloads of police in tactical armor retaliated by aggressively shutting down the bars, with the worst reported incident at the Elephant Walk, a gay bar at the corner of 18th and Castro. Customers were dragged from the bar and beaten by the police despite not being involved in the riots. The officers also trashed the interior of the bar and broke windows. Eyewitnesses reported the police were "totally out of control" as they randomly attacked people on the street and those who had taken shelter in the Elephant Walk.

The next night, May 22, 4,000 people gathered in the Castro area to celebrate what would have been Harvey Milk's birthday. The event had been planned long before the Civic Center riot. Mayor Feinstein ordered the police to stay out of the area. They were allowed one observation post so they could move in if trouble erupted. Between 250 to 300 gay volunteers monitored the crowds and helped keep the celebration peaceful. The celebration happened without incident.

Author's Notes

My use of "gay" vs. LGBTQ+ in my story

Part of my story occurred in the 1950s and early 1960s. This was years before Stonewall and the movements for LGBTQ+ equality. At that time, there were no rainbow flags, no PRIDE marches, no Marriage Equality, and we had very few of the freedoms our community enjoys today.

In those years before I was "out," we were "gay men" and "lesbians" to each other and to our friends. We were "faggots," "queers," and "dykes" to those who despised us.

For my story to ring authentic, I chose to use the term "gay" (and not LGBTQ+) to reflect those times. My use of "gay" may be seen by some as "politically incorrect." However, it reflects my reality and is grounded in my lived experience.

The Clouds

> *As mentioned in my story, I carefully watched the local newspapers for a report about the alleged destruction of the bar, but I found nothing. While writing my story, I researched The Honolulu Advertiser and The Honolulu Star Bulletin archives. Despite spending countless hours perusing newspaper archives, I came up empty handed. However, I learned The Clouds was under new management during the summer of 1964. I don't know if there was any connection between this change and the brawl. I speculate the bar owners didn't pursue the incident further as raising concerns with authorities could have jeopardized their liquor license.*
>
> *My curiosity led me to research what the passage of 60 years had brought to the block where The Clouds was located. The old two-story buildings were replaced by high-rises. One of the new buildings, the Waikiki Grand Hotel, sits where The Clouds once stood. I was delighted to learn the second floor became the home of Hula's Bar and Lei Stand, an LGBTQ+ bar featuring male dancers and drag shows. Hulu's opened in 1974, 10 years after The Clouds was trashed by the "men in dresses."*

Jim (he/him) had an interest in writing at an early age but not the confidence. That came later. At age 68, he published his first book, Love, Your Mother—Like It or Not *(www.amazon.com/dp/0692014470). A novel,* Tangled Webs *(www.amazon.com/dp/1737566400), inspired by that memoir, was released in 2022, when he was 80. Jim was a story coach for Paul Iarrobino's recent anthology,* COVIDOLOGY

(<u>www.ourboldvoices.com/covidology</u>). *He continues to write and his projects include: short stories, a sequel to* Tangled Webs *and a new novel about the gay experience in 1963. Jim lived in Hawaii, San Francisco, and Portland. He now lives in Bellingham, Washington.*

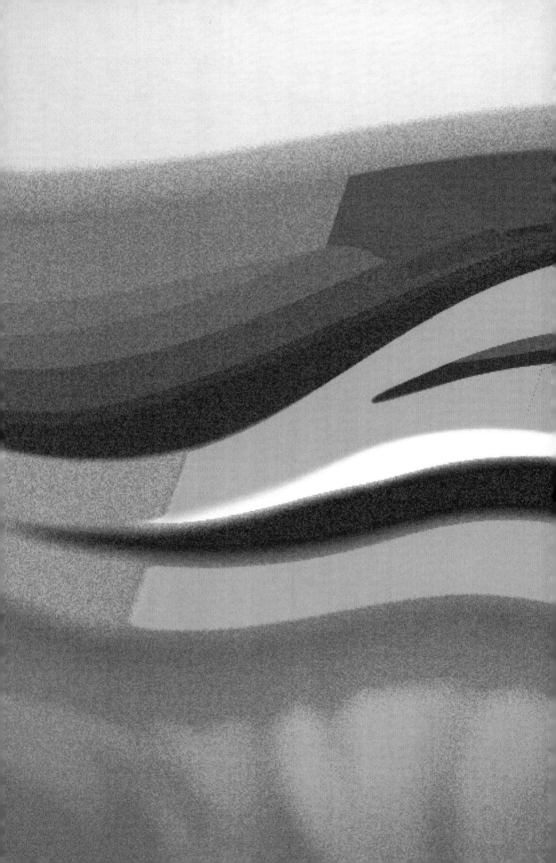

"Shorts Story"

by Brett Iarrobino

The gay agenda is rolled shorts!" A friend playfully **leaves the rallying cry under my Instagram post.** I don't recall what I've shared with the world to invoke such a reply, but this comment is etched with some permanence into my brain. It always reminds me of a prediction and evokes in my mind an image. I'm sure it's July or August in the photo: my shirt not quite completely buttoned, a warm smile draped across my face. And my shorts, as my digital comrade reminds me, are carefully cuffed, two identical halos framing my hairy set of white legs beneath. It's a fashion choice that's now carried me dutifully through many summers, an important routine of dressing myself once New England temperatures draw us out to beaches and lakes.

I find joyous humor in the fact that rolled shorts play a defining role in my relationship with queerness, a watershed moment in how I appear and present myself to others. What started as an incredulous exploration of a brand-new look snowballed into a crucial stepping stone, becoming my ritual before leaving the house. It's part of a telling and transparent suit of armor, an invitation to those who are perceptive and literate in visual queerness, and it announces my proud membership in their communities.

I am no historian. I haven't the faintest idea where the act of rolling up the ends of one's shorts into neat cuffs ranks in the pantheon of gay fashion. I only know that this simple routine revolutionized my understanding and expanded my self-expression. For nearly two decades, I floundered helplessly with an assortment of button fasteners and zipper pulls. I struggled with a sea of absurdly unnecessary pockets that I wish I could redistribute to all the pocketless women's pants. I dreaded the overhang of too-long shorts running over my knees. What once felt so busy and bulky below my waistline disappeared with each ascending roll of my cuffs.

Whereas I can remember every prosaic detail of when I came out with incredible precision, I can't clearly recall the first time I rolled up my shorts. Instead, it's much easier to talk about the grim wardrobe decisions that preceded my choice to roll my cuffs. For 12 years and change, how I dressed was a depressing cocktail of confusion, apathy, and unrelenting insecurity. As I trudged through adolescence, my brain slowly connected the dots that pointed arrows toward my queerness. My sense of style, however, barely moved a muscle despite these feelings.

I can only describe this aforementioned "style" as a parade of plain tees, basketball shorts, and a slim rotation of sweatshirts. The sweatshirts were worn so noticeably often that a teacher once half-jokingly asked me how often they were seeing the inside of a washing machine. Not only was I closeted, but the closet in which I hid held a decidedly underwhelming wardrobe. Like a fetal, gay variant of E.T., I concealed myself amongst the same, safe rotation of "outfits." They hung lifelessly in my closet showing the wear and tear from routine trips to school. The closet is isolating enough for queer kids. For some reason, I refused to cultivate a closet that offered up any originality. My revolution would not be televised, and my individuality would not stand out.

Looking back, I realize my adolescent years were comically underwhelming, and not so much because I was still grappling with what it meant to be gay or that my gayness felt so inevitably hard to face. It's more so that my journey through high school was not spent cowering in bathroom stalls or exiled at a reclusive lunch table. My high school life was not lonesome! I had real companionship with others who consistently proved themselves to be safe and reliable humans. They would welcome whatever labels I might someday publicly align with. That same patience and prospective compassion extended to my immediate family. Looking back, my family must have been anticipating a special announcement from me that would inevitably make its rounds.

Because of these real connections—both with my prototype chosen family and the real deal, my oft-supportive birth family—I was often able to give myself authentically to others in many settings and contexts. I found a sort of self-aware humor in the silent confusion I often evoked from others, prancing through life as gay as a mesh t-shirt I wouldn't ever dream of wearing. I found ways to laugh *with* my friends at the curiously restricted assortment of garments I could pull out of my closet. I tried to assuage myself that I was happy with my aesthetic countenance. Attempting a soft launch of queerness by confiding in others that I thought I might be bisexual, I still felt myself feigning coziness in that same woeful closet. I gaslighted my brain with C.S. Lewis-style[1] fantasies and into thinking my fabric prison sprawled out into something liberating and sustainable.

Materially, nothing had changed, of course. I was still hiding behind a compulsory buzzcut; cutting shears ripping into my dark Italian wool every time I played chicken with the growth. My everyday, all-occasion footwear continued to be a pair of bulky sneakers. Through all this, I was rounding out my adolescence and chugging my way towards an inevitable great escape into queer joy. But still, I let my self-expression limp behind, indignantly determined to be a late bloomer, struggling to keep up with the patterned shirts and sartorial sensations that I knew brought me comfort and pleasure.

I came out just before I graduated from high school, for reasons many of us know, as we nod our heads while we silently read these stories. I was tired of lying to myself about who I was and tired of denying myself the normalcy I knew I could find in being gay. Thankfully, the horror stories of such ordeals are not my story to tell—partly because I was raised by responsible and level-headed humans, and also because I had primed my parents to receive such trivial and unsurprising news since insisting on dressing in princess gowns through my terrible twos. The irony of this is not lost on me: that the toddler version of me found the strength to dress authentically and enthusiastically, only to lose such confidence in the transition of childhood and adolescence somewhere along the way. At 3, I was holding court with girls, babbling about exhilarating fantasies of witches and evil queens. By 17, I could barely spit out my sexuality while hiding in a burlap sack of sweats and sneakers. Being socialized as a man in this country saw my coven and confidence disappear. But this crucial first step in admitting who I am started the process of doing right by the diva of my youth.

I was relieved to finish the job of coming out and glad to finally share such a silly non-secret with friends and family. But I could feel my patience with fashion finally evaporating. I remember it felt like taking enormous leaps of faith when I traded sweatshirts for the occasional sweater. Supplanting sweatpants with banal light blue jeans. These old favorites suddenly felt like vestiges of my old life, and I felt okay about leaving them behind.

Undeniably, my sense of self was now no longer in unison with how I wanted to show myself to everyone else, and remedial pilgrimages to thrift stores and girlfriends' advisory phone calls were frequently prescribed. I began using apps with algorithms smart enough to know I was gay before I was ready to say it out loud. This meant that I had spent years absorbing alluring men's fashion from my phone screen that went directly into the same area of my brain that harbored forbidden dopamine rushes—rushes for the men and for the skin beneath the clothes they were modeling. Pocket t-shirts, slim-fitting pants, and above all else, the coveted short shorts—outfits I imagined myself wearing in alternative realities. Those realities were becoming more plausible as I realized that my style could be something signature. With a long way to go towards my authentic aesthetic, I finally secured a roadmap to the imaginary fitting room where I could try on these same outfits. Slowly but surely, I was building a wardrobe that felt more reflective of my newfound embrace of and confidence in queerness.

Despite my progress, I still started college as a nervous kid and feeling unsure of the one and only body I owned that would carry me through the world. I still settled for a limited collection of jeans, khakis, and much-too-baggy cargo shorts. The desire to blend in was fleeting, though, and I suddenly traded my homogeneous and predictable *high school community* for a visibly queer *student body*. My peers' fashion choices ranged from profound to camp to downright absurd. And they all shared a common purpose: they magnified my complete inability to keep up with the couture of my subculture. The outfits I saw at parties and debaucherous evenings cut through my timid fashion sense with tremendous fervor. I felt an unnamed exasperation with how long it had taken me to see this literal and metaphorical color spectrum of clothing as normal. I felt as though I was finally living on my own terms. I was surrounded by literally countless queer people moving and shaking their way through a new world, and I felt my excitement for life return. I no longer kissed boys out of desperation. And as I crossed my legs and raised my brows with a well-measured dose of femininity, a light turned on in me. Again, I found myself yearning for reinvention, for greater equilibrium between the illumination within me and around me.

It wasn't enough to wear clothes I connected with and believed in. I needed something that reminded the world how proud I was to be feminine and to love men. To let the world know I was different in the way I talked and loved as compared to other people. I needed to trade in cargo shorts for the visual equivalent of a lilted voice.

Enter my patron saint of euphoric queer fashion, the short shorts! Much like my struggle to recall when I first looked at the same gender with desire, I cannot specifically remember when I first bundled the end of my shorts to rest in a crown above knee level. I do, however, remember the first time someone noticed my rolled cuffs: my sister. Joining my family on a campus visit, and before she leaned in to hug me goodbye, my sister asked incredulously if my shorts were rolled up. My roommate explained the obviousness of the fashion statement before I could answer saying, "Of course they are! Do you realize how gay this campus is?" My sister, ever the ally, shrugged and finished our embrace.

The easy answers to why rolled shorts loom as large as they do in my journey to self-discovery is the femininity of the garment and also how profoundly boring men's fashion can be. The deeper truth is that losing some inches on the bottom of my summer apparel was a game-changer. It ushered in all sorts of new apparel choices: patterned button-downs, slim-fit trousers, and oh-so-subtle cross-dressing items that I wouldn't have dreamt of wearing before the critical cuff.

A friend once politely asked me about the practice of cuffing shorts and its personal meaning. I tried my best to articulate how burdened and awkward I felt when saddled with wearing shorts that simply felt "too long" (read: too masculine). Losing the morose flapping of long, drooping fabric from the pant legs of my shorts—occasionally so protracted the pant legs greeted the edge of my shins while walking—was like shedding a weighted blanket. Ditching the stifling parts of dressing myself paved the way for more choices that felt bolder and sweeter. These new looks were my advertisements for the warmth and gregariousness I could offer a room. A plaid turtleneck made from crossing fuchsia and crepe pink, yellow bottoms flashing the same bright shade as the highlighter on my desk, or a cyan blouse with faint, outlined carnations crocheted across the stripes.

Today, I catch up with all the colors I hid from but longed for back in my days of lurking behind safe grays and dark blues.

I didn't feel I could subscribe to homosexuality, queerness, and the unbridled joy derived from presenting myself as fruity without a legible aesthetic to back it up. And as I rolled my shorts and feminized the closet that once held me captive, I felt myself simply getting happier with the results. The breeze on my partially exposed thighs was as euphoric and affirming as locking lips with a guy. With just one slight tweak below the waist, I began to reveal more of myself to the world, literally and metaphorically.

I would never reduce queerness to a material concern, but at the risk of invoking a contemporary buzzword, I do believe it is a "vibe." Telegraphing myself as someone who is comfortable straddling lines between masculinity and fem-ininity, my relationships with others tenderly grow around it, too. I feel this growth professionally, when an employer unflinchingly defends our right to dress however we please. I feel it personally when a woman leaving the grocery store benevolently whistles at my run through the sidewalk. "Love the legs!" she cheers with a safe smile.

Years have gone by and I'm still rolling my shorts. I now frequently purchase women's shorts, which means it's not the vital task it once was. My self-expression journey continues to materialize in exciting ways, and I remain steadfast in tracing my current aesthetics to the ground zero event of discovering that queerness can exist in cloth.

Not long ago, I bought my first romper. Days after wearing it to work, a colleague gifted me one she had ordered for herself. Ultimately, she didn't love it as much as she thought she would. Giving me the romper she said, "It's cute, it's summery, and it's colorful. I totally thought of you!" Like many other similar moments, her conviction as she shared this sentiment reminded me that this style of mine is not just aesthetically endearing but one that simply made sense for who I am. The light inside me is, at long last, in balance with the vessel that holds it. I don't know which fruity gentleman first discovered that our shorts need not reach the end of our knees—but my liberated calves thank him for it. Living in the closet is already gauche enough; it is merely equity in action when queer people get first dibs on and snatch up its most desirable offerings. We deserve the loveliest linens and denim and nylons—after having hidden ourselves for so long where these offerings hang—before we found our footing and learned to strut in style.

Endnotes

1 C.S. Lewis, author of *The Chronicles of Narnia* children's book series, where a large, ornate wardrobe magically transports its users into a fantastical new country.

Brett (they/them) is a writer and educator in Worcester, Massachusetts. Their playwriting has received professional development with the Kennedy Center after placing nationally for the 2021 John Cauble Award for Outstanding Short Play. Their writing on teaching and pedagogy has been published in The ALAN Review *(alan-ya.org/publications/the-alan-review-tar) of the National Council of Teachers of English (ncte.org). Brett holds a B.A. in English and Theatre Arts from Clark University and an M.A. in Teaching from Clark's Adam Institute for Urban Teaching and School Practice. Brett is also a proud co-founder of the Worcester Writers' Collective, a nonprofit working out of Worcester's Jean McDonough Arts Center (jmacworcester.org).*

Out of the Margins: Living in Visibility

visibility (noun): the state or fact of being able to be seen

By Tom Finch

n May 2023, I came out as a gay man to my fourth grade students. It happened spontaneously while I was teaching a health and human development lesson.

Who knew? I never thought the day would come. Yet, it did and in the most organic of ways.

My school district adopted a new health curriculum. It doesn't sugarcoat a thing. It explicitly covers anatomy, it's gender-inclusive, and it's a breath of fresh air. It talks about the different types of attraction between people, and the words gay, transgender, queer, and gender-fluid are all factually used. This is done in a developmentally-appropriate context because, well, it's Portland, Oregon. While some places attempt to erase our progress by policy or by law, Portland is beautifully progressive. The city is a safe haven and protects what so many fought for before us, and many continue to fight for now: our visibility.

Things were going smoothly. The kids were engaged. Then, the words just popped out of my mouth. At that moment, my emotions took over. I just went with the flow and let the possible consequences born of past experience be damned.

"Well," I started, "I'm gay. I love a man, and he's my boyfriend."

"What the heck just happened?" I thought to myself with bewilderment.

One student looked at me and smiled. Another had a twinkle in her eye and a knowing smile, as if to say: *I thought so. I already knew, buddy.* Kids are so perceptive. A parent later wrote an email thanking me for coming out and for modeling visibility for her two gender-fluid children. I cried tears of relief and release. Who knew this day would come? After my past experiences as a gay educator, I took to heart the power of visibility both as privilege and responsibility.

I refuse to become invisible ever again. I long ago chose visibility as a path within me. I'm out at work. I'm out to my family. I'm out to my friends. I hold my man's hand in public. I kiss him without even thinking twice as to set or setting at any given moment. My privilege as a White cisgender male in Portland, Oregon, always me to do this. I feel secure in knowing that local law and ordinance protect me—and me especially. Many do not enjoy such protection. Would I feel the same way about visibility if I were a gay person of color? My answer might very well differ. This privilege of mine must be acknowledged as I tell my story.

Who could ever forget Gary? During my years growing up in Des Moines, Iowa, Gary was our family hairdresser. Gary was a cool guy. He rode a motorcycle, he wore leather, and he always looked like he meant business. We chatted and laughed as he styled my hair. He was patient with me as I came up with my various and now amusing hairstyles.

Before we moved away to Cleveland, Ohio, in 1988, Gary gave me my final haircut. I was 13 years old. He was cutting my asymmetrical bangs and taming my then curly hair into submission. Who would be able to manage my hair now that we were moving away? I realized how much I would miss Gary and our conversations. It was this haircut that planted a seed within me.

During this last haircut and referring to our previous conversations, Gary nonchalantly said, "Phil isn't just my

roommate, Tom. As a gay man, now you know before you go."
I felt like one of my future students. I just looked at Gary, my
eyes wide in the mirror, and I didn't utter a word. I was filled
with emotions, both confusing and exhilarating. I didn't yet
understand the power of having a role model, a visible face
to put into context the urges I felt inside me. I knew this
fundamentally. I never saw Gary again after that, not even
when I later looked for him at the salon as a young, out adult.
I wanted to thank him for recognizing something within me
that I couldn't yet see for myself.

Cleveland, Ohio, of the 1990s was a conservative city
peppered with clandestine pockets of liberal minds and with
organizations that were accepting of queer youth. Seeking
and finding this sense of community was an instinct I felt
and couldn't deny. I made hushed phone calls to the city's
Gay/Lesbian Center that revealed the existence of a youth
group called PRYSM[1] (Pride and Respect for Youth in the
Sexual Minority). Led by compassionate and caring adults,
it was located in a worn brick building on West 29th Street
near the Cuyahoga River's meandering path through the
downtown center. It offered a refuge of understanding and
empathy to young people struggling with their sexual identity. As my sexuality blossomed, I learned how to navigate
through tensions at home and received guidance on how to
deal with the sometimes hostile world of high school. My
own high school did not have a Gender and Sexuality Alliance, a group that assisted youth seeking support and guidance. It wasn't yet the time. The field of public education

wasn't unilaterally ready. And so, people sought and found community in another environment.

"I'll never come out!" I remember exclaiming emphatically during a PRYSM meeting. "My parents and family must never know! It's just better that way!"

"You might change your mind one day," said one leader knowingly while another leader looked on with dismay. The two group leaders, by their own visibility and openness, showed us how to face adversity head on. I didn't understand it then, but their actions spoke louder than words, and in doing so, they murmured words of wisdom to me gained through their own experiences. Their words also held a bit of a prophecy as I did change my mind and decided to come out to my parents and sister in August 1992. A high school friend in whom I had confided chose to share my secret without my permission with other students at the school. When I found out, I knew that this information, no matter how upsetting or disruptive, must reach the ears of my family from my own mouth and not from the mouths of others. Perhaps my hand was forced a bit. Perhaps it was just the right and predestined time. Regardless, the cards were visibly placed on the table, and there was no going back.

Leandro, my friend and a fellow PRYSM group member, placed his cards on the table in a similar fashion for his family to see. Leandro, like me, was 18. He lived in the next Cleveland suburb just east of mine and attended a boarding school tucked in the rolling hills. Leandro was born in Argentina and spoke Spanish as well as English. He had smoldering dark eyes and the manners of a gentleman. Leandro and I became fast friends and soon bonded over our common threads: conservative fathers, upcoming college applications, and our shared need to escape the confines of our loving, if controlling, families. We wanted to spread our wings. In short order, we began meeting at a local coffeehouse. We borrowed our parents' cars and drove over to each other's houses to smoke late-night cigarettes on the driveway. We chatted, we muttered about our annoying siblings, and gushed over a cute newcomer to our weekly support group.

Together, we would carpool to the Gay/Lesbian Center every Saturday in order to connect with this little community. And with every meeting we began to realize that visibility needed to be a part of our future. My parents knew Leandro since I'd introduced him during a late-night driveway visit. They weren't too thrilled that I found a sidekick in gayness. I didn't care in the least. Leandro was a kindred spirit when I needed one the most. We both understood the challenges each of us faced in terms of initial acceptance and family support. We also both understood that the road ahead might not be easy or kind. A universal common denominator of humanity is to fear what we do not automatically understand—cognitively or emotionally.

One Saturday in late April of 1993 our group leader mentioned the March on Washington[2]. Leandro and I vowed that we would watch it on TV together if we could. As it turned out, we ended up each having to watch from our own homes. I don't recall exactly why we were unable to watch it together. However, I'll always recall the lump in my throat when I turned on the television, then called Leandro on the phone, wrapping the telephone cord around my finger with nervous energy. Together, over the wall-mounted rotary telephone wires, Leandro and I commented on the throngs of people on the lawn beneath the Washington monument and the joyful people dancing to music while wrapped in rainbow pride flags. Together, Leandro and I watched visibility in action knowing that we were part of a larger community. A community that, albeit not always visible in all places at all times, still existed. Together, we listened with one ear for approaching footsteps of family members and with one hand on the TV dial in order to change the channel if needed. Neither one of us wanted to deal with the questions from our families nor the potential for drama. Both of us needed to be fully present in the moment. We were together yet physically apart. We absorbed the display of visibility on the national stage before us. Both of us watching at the same time through the same medium, both watching the legions of people brave enough to stand up and say, "I, too, exist."

We both stood up a little straighter after that day, Leandro and I. Together, we then resolved to lead more visible lives. We held conversations more frequently with our well-meaning parents who, at the time, were still biased. We didn't apologize for making others uncomfortable with the topic. We went from meeting at coffee houses to sneaking into the downtown gay bars hoping no one asked for our IDs. We made plans for college the following year, wondering which state schools would be safest for LGBTQ+ students. We included visibility as a guideline for our respective futures.

Leandro and I graduated high school, and I headed to Miami University in Oxford, Ohio. We kept in touch as we both started our freshman years at our respective universities. In 1997, a section of the AIDS Quilt[3] was displayed at my university. On one panel the name "Gary" was quilted in large letters surrounded by written tributes and a few photos. The red velvet cordons around the quilt kept visitors away from the panels enough so that I couldn't make out the faces in the photos or read the writing on the panel other than the name.

I wondered if it could be Gary, the man who knew I was gay before I realized it myself. The man who understood me and planted a seed of awareness in me. To this day, that question remains unanswered. The memory of Gary's courage, as shown through the way he lived his life with visibility, is still very present within me.

Graduation came in May 1998, and back to Cleveland I went to begin my teaching career. How happy I was to be in the same town as Leandro again, yet it wasn't for long. Leandro moved from Ohio to Oregon. I followed two years later, but we nonetheless lost touch as the years passed and our connection changed. Our Saturday carpool drives to PRYSM and late-night driveway conversations became a distant memory. Yet, we maintained visibility in our lives. We made a choice to relocate to a region in which visibility is celebrated and encouraged.

My own path towards visibility as a gay teen began with Gary's coming out moment to me and the way he modeled visibility. Five years later, I was forever changed when I watched the events of April 25, 1993, in Washington, DC. On this day, thousands upon thousands of brave people participated in the March on Washington where they demonstrated an unwavering visibility fueled by their strength in numbers. Widely covered by the media, the events, performances, and speeches were broadcast into homes across the nation and the world. Some viewers and listeners expressed hostility and scorn. For others, though, many seeds were planted and nurtured on that day. My personal choice to be out and visible in all elements of my current day-to-day life is a result of such seeds that were planted within me over time.

And then there is Leandro. I still think of him from time to time. I often wonder if he fully realizes his significant role in my path towards visibility. I also wonder, if we ever meet again, would our shared experiences allow us to pick up where we left off? I hope our paths will cross again someday.

If only I could wave a metaphorical wand. I'd bend time and space in order to manifest a meeting of important moments and people in my life past and present. I would conjure the three of us: Gary, Leandro, and me. We would suddenly find ourselves at a well-worn and well-loved Portland locale. We'd swap stories, reminisce, and remember. I'd heartily thank them over pints of locally-crafted beer or maybe a shot, then I'd buy them each the next round as well. I'd thank them for planting those seeds of visibility in me, perhaps intentionally or perhaps unknowingly. I'd let them know of the ripple they created and how it grew over time into this personal commitment to visibility within me. As with ripples across a still pond, the effects of visibility upon others grow and wane, bounce and reflect, then fade and begin again.

It's now summertime, and my students bounced out the door and into the sunny afternoon about three weeks ago. Around my desk are small relics of the school year: a card, a worksheet, a rogue sticker. My thoughts turn to them. I wonder if coming out to my students within the context of the lesson might have cast forth some small seeds of visibility to a student trying to find their way. Perhaps it did, and perhaps it didn't. I don't know, nor is it for me to know. In the meantime, I'll just continue to walk, to be, and to love visibly during my time on our planet. It's the least that I can do to honor the ones who guided me toward this moment.

Endnotes

1 A gay-straight alliance, gender-sexuality alliance (GSA), or queer-straight alliance (QSA) is a student-led or community-based group. They are found in middle schools,

high schools, colleges, and universities primarily in the United States and Canada. Gay-straight alliances provide a safe and supportive environment for LGBTQ+ students and allies.

2 Formally known as the March on Washington for Lesbian, Gay, and Bi Equal Rights and Liberation, this gathering in Washington, DC, of between 800,000 and 1,000,000 people on April 25, 1993, was one of the largest protests in the history of the United States. Calls to action made by organizers included funding for HIV/AIDS research and education, legal rights and protections for people identifying as LGBTQ+, and reproductive freedom and choice.

3 This textile memorial to over 94,000 people consists of more than 48,000 panels and weighs over 54 tons. It started in 1985 as a way for surviving family members and friends to remember loved ones at a time when fear and stigma led to burial discrimination and refusal to inter remains. Each panel is three feet by six feet. It has been shown in various locations over the years, both in its entirety and in traveling sections.

Author's Note

It's hard to define a memory along conventional lines. Some recollections are concrete, some are abstract, some very detailed, and some are fleeting. They come rushing back when we least expect: scents, sounds, sights, the feelings experienced within a moment. This was my experience while writing about my own journey of visibility. Memories long filed away and almost for-

gotten were suddenly reanimated with a new vibrancy, almost forcing my eyes closed in order to gaze further within.

In my mind's eye, I can see the low, two-story, brick building that housed Cleveland's Gay/Lesbian Center. I recall the angled windows around entrances and the creaky floors. I remember the musty smell of the basement meeting rooms and the smoky smell of the bar next door. I am flooded with the small flickers within the greater flame of this memory, and it comes alive once again. It is as if writing this personal narrative has become a time machine. I visualize my 18-year-old self, watching myself chatter excitedly with other youth group members outside the Center, their faces blurred in my memories until the moment of reactivation. I wish I could whisper reassurances into the ear of my younger self, saying visibility wouldn't always be an easy path to take, and that those moments of difficulty truly were and are just one more plate in the armor.

After committing these memories and ruminations on visibility to printed text, curiosity prevailed, and I found myself wondering about the Center. Was it still in the low, two-story, brick building on West 28th Street? Back then, it was almost invisible among the old retail spaces and warehouses unless one knew exactly where to look.

My internet search revealed an image of the old space as well as an image of the new LGBT Center of Greater Cleveland, a soaring new building of glass and concrete clearly visible from blocks away. And so, the two buildings became a metaphor for the power of visibility in the world. The building housing the center evolved from nondescript to one commanding the attention and respect of passers-by. The old building provided the foundation for the new one just as the small moments of visibil-

ity in my earlier life led me to a commitment to visibility in the present and the future.

Tom (he/him) lives and works in Portland, Oregon as an elementary educator. When he isn't sharing corny jokes with his students, he is mastering the art and science of crockpot cooking, perplexing his incredibly patient and loving family, and finding every reason to delay returning to the gym. Tom shares his life with an amazing man, Chris, and a grumpy cockatiel, Noor, both of whom somehow tolerate his idiosyncrasies. He enjoys travel, languages, kayaking, and lifelong learning.

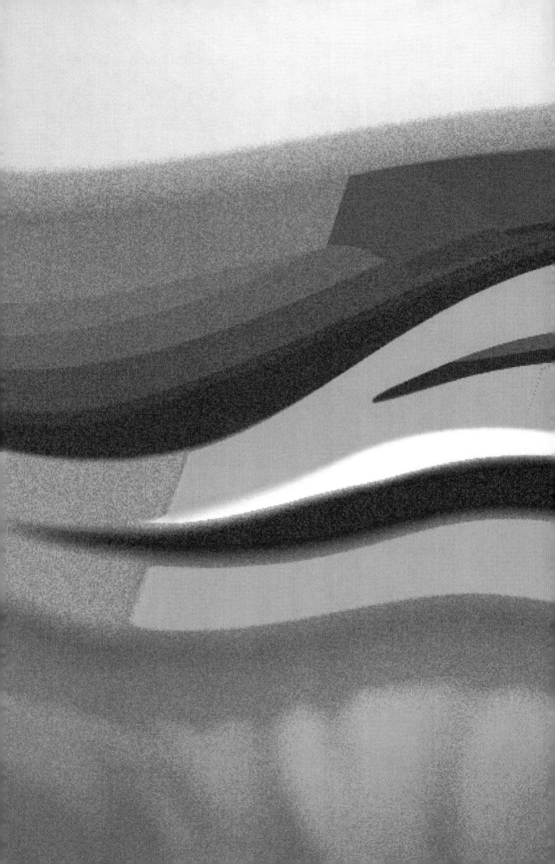

Learning to Breathe

By Scott Strickland

I grew up in an emotionless family that expressed themselves with flat monotone voices. When my mother laughed it was always at someone else's misfortune. I still remember being startled by the sound of her laughter. She was a classic narcissist and Machiavellian psychopath. The world centered around her and her needs. Everyone else was incidental, including me. Other people were present only to the degree that they fluffed her ego and were easily, and frequently, discarded. I was to be out of sight and out of mind. She never touched my father who was physically absent most of the time and emotionally absent all of the time. My mother had an affair, divorced my father, and vanished from my life. I was 14 years old at the time. I spent the next four years living at home in a strange isolation. I was totally alone in a world where other people were some kind of abstraction. They were there but not part of my reality. If I was gone, or dead, would anyone know?

I knew that I was gay after I discovered a passage in a 1950s Encyclopedia Britannica under "homosexual." Even in the sterile prose of a mid-century encyclopedia I knew that was me. I also knew it was socially unacceptable, and I packed that knowledge away along with anything else that resembled an emotion. Just like my mother, I was a faceless monolith. I also felt an underlying anxiety that someone might see a crack in my facade. Maintaining my cloak of stoicism was an all-pervading obsession. "Why are you always so nervous?" I heard constantly from people I was speaking to. Doctors always commented on my fast pulse. I felt like I could never exhale—or relax.

School was my sanctuary. I loved being in class and never missed a day after a bout of mumps in the third grade. I was interested in knowledge simply for the sake of knowing. I took all of the classes I could and did well even without trying. Everyone else complained about homework, but I got As just by going to class. When I started doing homework, I became the smart guy, the one to go to for help with classes. "That's Scott. He is really smart. Weird but smart." Teaching became part of my identity. It was my first taste of feeling that I was of value to someone else. Physical Education (PE) was a nightmare. I was fascinated with the locker rooms, but they felt too dangerous to me. Participating in organized competitive sports was impossible. I didn't give a damn about winning anything, and I despised competition. The teachers (coaches) were only interested in the athletes, and the rest of us were ridiculed. Even individual sports were impossible for me. I nearly drowned when I tried to learn to swim. I needed to learn to breathe to swim, but just like the rest of my days, I felt like I could never exhale, and I was drowning in life.

College was a seismic shift. I landed in the perfect place seemingly by total chance. No one helped me find the right place. My family wanted me gone, and they were delighted that I found a place out of state and out of mind. My mother dropped me off at the front door and drove away. She had been emotionally absent from my life for 18 years and now was vanishing through the oak grove in front of the college to the main road. I turned my back on her before she even closed the car door. It would be years before I saw her again. I felt like I had run away from home.

There I was on campus. Living in a dorm room with a man. Surrounded by other men. I had absolutely no social skills that could help me navigate my way forward. What do you do when there is an invitation to a party? If a woman talks to you, does she want to go on a date? If a man talks to you, does he know you are gay? I never understood social conversations and was clueless about social cues. I misunderstood innuendos and read threats into every conversation. I was anxious all of the time and hyperventilated any time a conversation lasted more than a few minutes. I was exhausted by social interactions and avoided them at all costs.

Thanksgiving, the first school holiday, was coming. I had never done anything for Thanksgiving before and never considered doing anything now. A well-meaning dorm mate asked me to come to his family's house for dinner. I reluctantly agreed to go. Once there, I was in a roomful of people I didn't know. I felt trapped. After a few awkward conversations, I went to the bathroom, vomited, and left. My friend never spoke to me again.

On the upside, I was enthralled with my classes. Everyone was interested in the subjects without the noisy, mindless idiots that lurked in the back of every high school classroom. PE meant horseshoes and handball with other uncoordinated geeks, and there were no intimidating coaches watching over us. Still, everyday felt like I was navigating through a minefield, and I looked for every opportunity to escape. The library had quiet rooms with no others around. I took refuge there often, and I could relax enough to breathe. As I peered out the windows at the commons, I felt like I was watching a movie in which I had no role. But things were about to change.

I was a super student. I tested out of classes. As in everything, I thought up new classes and took them as independent study. I got scholarships for tuition, and tutoring jobs made up for the rest. The go-to-guy for tutoring. I was a teaching assistant in classes I was taking as a student. Teaching seemed to give me a sense of value, but I felt like none of it was real. If I continued to teach, everyone would eventually figure out that I was a total fake, a fabrication, a fraud. More than once I planned to leave school before I was discovered. Thoughts of suicide occasionally drifted through my reality. Then came Organic Chemistry.

Organic Chemistry was as natural for me as breathing should have been, and it was a lot easier. Home Ec students had difficulty with Organic Chemistry. I put together a curriculum that taught Organic Chemistry using a kitchen and common ingredients from the pantry. Using my curriculum, the Home Ec students started passing and then cooked the rest of the class dinner once a week. What a deal! Physics, computer programming, math, and biology were simple for me, almost intuitive. Going to classes was now pure pleasure, and learning was fulfilling for me in ways I hadn't experienced before. Just as in high school, I enjoyed learning simply for the sake of learning. The rest of college life—fraternities, sports, parties, dorm life—passed before my eyes like a jerky old black and white movie. I watched, but I didn't participate.

Then came Nancy and Stephen. They were each other's lab partners in the Organic Chemistry class where I tutored. Nancy was the stellar teaching assistant in biology and had a jolly laugh. Stephen was two years younger than Nancy and me. They laughed and joked together with a comfortable banter. I was inexplicably drawn to them. They made me laugh, and they seemed welcoming. Nancy lived off campus and invited me and Stephen for dinner. I remembered the disaster four years earlier at Thanksgiving, but I didn't feel threatened, so I accepted. We laughed, talked, made dinner, and relaxed. I now had two friends, and my life pivoted. It was the first time that I exhaled.

The ensuing months with Nancy and Stephen were a vivid kaleidoscope in my memory. We gathered with others, went to movies, ate at restaurants, traveled, studied, and acted in school plays. We embraced each other as three inseparable friends with shared interests and unconditional acceptance. We were a trio that others saw as a little bit nerdy and awkward. We were comfortable in our differences, and subliminally we knew we were damaged in our own ways like birds with broken wings. Nancy was an overweight science and math student (not subjects for women in the 1970s). On the surface, Stephen was strikingly handsome, externally confident, a dancer, an actor, and intellectually brilliant. Even as a sophomore, he was taking upper-level classes and was on a full scholarship to go to medical school. He came from a small town and was strangely secretive about his family. He occasionally mocked his parents and their conservative religious convictions but did so in a way that made it clear we were not to ask more questions.

Stephen and I performed in several school plays and spent long days rehearsing together. We occasionally went out to eat together afterward and talked for hours. He won a state championship for ballet, performed in musicals and plays, and sang. Stephen graduated at the top of his high school class and was the only person that I knew who had a perfect SAT score. He knew more useless details than I did, and I loved useless details. Spending time with Stephen and Nancy gave me a light, dreamy feeling, and I looked forward to seeing them. One evening after dinner, Stephen touched my arm. It felt like much more than just a touch, and a lightning storm erupted in my body. I don't remember ever feeling my body before that. The feeling passed, and I hid it away like a forbidden secret.

Stephen and I developed a tradition of eating chocolate-covered coffee beans, which felt like a daring thing to do for two hopelessly naive young men. The caffeine stimulated our conversation, and I felt an unfamiliar warmth. I had never felt that kind of feeling and certainly not where I was feeling it. We discussed Lady Chatterley's Lover by D. H. Lawrence, which we considered to be pornography in our sexually-repressed lives. Our conversations became progressively more intimate, at first about the book, and then about ourselves. For several months our meetings were like entering a warm, humid cloud of whirling breezes. Stolen glances. Intentional touches. Vague sexual references. One indirect reference to erections almost segued us into something more, but we stopped short.

One Tuesday night everything settled slowly into place for us. Studying was over. We shared dinner at a local college hangout. After a little too much caffeine, we were alone in Stephen's single occupancy room. Suggestive chatter, as one of us lay back onto the pillow. Nervous unbuttoning. Shirts off. Pants. Hands to skin. Lips to lips. The painful awkwardness of the first time. A long crescendo finally ends in an ecstatic explosion. We shared some nervous laughter and giggling that quickly stopped as campus curfew approached. I wafted out the door, down the stairs, and across the quad. This was the last time that I was aware of any physical feelings below my neck. I took a deep breath of fresh Willamette Valley fall air. I was excitedly thinking about the Organic Chemistry lab the next day.

I bounded into class the next morning. Someone commented on my smile—he had never seen that before. Stephen wasn't there, which was odd since he was an otherwise obsessive-compulsive person. Hours passed. Finally, I saw him walking across the lawn. I waited by the door. He walked toward me but didn't make eye contact until the last minute. With a blank stare he muttered, "What you did was a sin. God will punish you," as he walked a few steps past me. He turned back and growled, "You never meant anything to me." That was the end, and the door snapped shut. I thought I was suffocating. We never spoke again. We would occasionally pass each other on campus as if the other person was a blank space on a black canvas.

I went back to my only familiar role. I was the awkward, smart kid who was useful as a teacher but otherwise had no real identity. I somehow survived college, graduate school, and decades of work. My relationships were infrequent and shallow. My lack of social skills and self-imposed isolation meant decades of bone-deep melancholy. I was totally alone, but almost miraculously I was saved from the health scourge of the 1980s: AIDS. So many people that I knew or worked with died, and yet I felt nothing. My life was a cold lead blanket that enveloped me for the next 30 years. I often felt like I was walking along the event horizon of a black hole, ready to be sucked into oblivion at any moment, and occasionally wishing I would be.

I moved to a different part of the country, and Nancy moved to another continent. We quickly lost contact. Many years later, we reconnected when a friend of hers was sitting next to me on an airplane flight. I reached out to Nancy, and we met for dinner at a local restaurant. "What happened to Stephen?" I asked in passing. Nancy and I were joyfully catching up on 30 years of being apart. I was expecting tales of Stephen's life and of his unbridled successes. Her normally jolly and pink cheeks turned stark white and stone cold. There was an uncomfortable pause, and in a quiet and measured tone Nancy replied, "He died." She continued, "Stephen died of AIDS 10 years ago." It was as if every molecule of oxygen left the room. My encroaching autonomic response blurred Nancy's features and reduced her voice to a thin, tinny noise echoing from the end of a long black tube. In time, the full story of Stephen's life and death would emerge, but for now we engaged in some uneasy pleasantries, and then we parted. Old feelings overpowered me, and I felt like I couldn't exhale. How could Stephen be dead?

Stephen's life was worse than I expected, but it followed an all-too-familiar storyline. He eventually came out as gay and fell headfirst into a life of alcohol, drugs, and anonymous sex. His charming personality and intelligence made him everyone's friend, and his striking good looks made him everyone's sex partner. He continued to be manipulated by his conservative parents and was occasionally sucked back into their religious torture chamber. He stumbled through medical school as the early symptoms of AIDS started to appear. He got a job in South Dakota but became too sick to continue. He returned to his family who took care of him in return for his renunciation of his sexuality and his rejoining the church. He apparently was cut off from all other contacts, and his family wouldn't speak of him. I visited his grave a few months later. "Forever in our hearts" was inscribed on his gravestone. Their hearts were not big enough to celebrate who he really was, but they were small enough to be complicit in his death.

Nancy and I maintained a warm relationship and leaned on each other as we struggled with our own demons for the next five years. Nevertheless, the same differences that made us friends years before were still there after being suppressed for decades. My social difficulties began to affect my behavior, which eventually led to illegal activity. After a failed suicide attempt, I went to prison for eight years. Nancy and I maintained a distant but supportive correspondence throughout my incarceration. Writing letters to her was therapy in itself and evolved into a type of support group that I organized for fellow prisoners. Prison offers no help and no chances for rehabilitation. With help from Nancy and a few supportive people on the outside, I began to dig out of 50 years of depression. There were many inmates in prison who suffered the same mental health problems that I did, and we banded together for support and mutual learning. Healing came in the most unexpected places. We put on plays, learned yoga and meditation, and read about Cognitive Behavioral Therapy. We pursued meaningful spiritual growth, joined Toastmasters, and taught other inmates basic GED skills. Most importantly, we held each other accountable for our crimes. Prison is a warehouse where naïve people learn to be better at committing crimes. But our small group insisted on focused self-improvement and tried to spread a positive message. When I left prison, I was a different person, a better person, with more empathy, altruism, and self-awareness.

Nancy made the 300-mile trip to prison to see me often. Just seeing her smile once a month and having a conversation free of prison drama helped me beyond comprehension. On her last visit, she revealed she was experiencing some turmoil at work. Her final letter implied that things were getting complicated and then I never heard from her again. Two years later Nancy took her own life. She spoke to me about my suicide attempt several times. I will never know if my suicide attempt influenced her decision. I will carry that burden forever.

Five years have passed since my release. With therapy, medications, acupuncture, and a loving support group, I am okay. I have learned how to breathe. I also learned how to take care of myself so that the darkness is never as deep. I do yoga, exercise, and meditate often. When the disembodied vacuum of depression starts to creep over me, I know it is time to stop and ask what is happening to me rather than stuffing my feelings deep inside. When someone offers a gentle hug, a half-smile, or genuine compassion, it reignites my joy and nudges me back on track.

When I replay the mental tapes of my life, it is like walking through my own personal graveyard. There is an entire section dedicated to my friends and colleagues who died of AIDS. How many lives would have been saved if there had been a robust public health response in 1980 instead of shaming and blaming? Hundreds of thousands of deaths lost to homophobia and ignorance. Stephen said once that he felt like he was chained to a cold metal pole, and when he tried to pull away, his parents and their inflexible religion would snap him back and tie him ever tighter. He died from a virus, but it was a death by proxy. Nancy was smart, assertive, and overweight. There was never a place for a woman like her in the rigid confines of society, and the mental health system was incapable of helping her. I am grateful for each breath and to be alive and hold space for their memories. I have a picture of Nancy, Stephen, and me making dinner and smiling in Nancy's tiny college apartment. We are less for having lost them. I had a small inscription engraved into a brick and placed near where we met. "Nancy '75, Scott '76, Stephen '78." They will be with me forever.

Author's Notes

On GRID/AIDS

The Gay Related Immune Deficiency, or GRID for short, is what they called AIDS at first. Morbidity and Mortality Weekly Report (MMWR) first reported it on June 5, 1981. People were dying of a new, rapidly-progressing disease. The report was alarming, but just a few years before, in 1976, another new disease killed 29, mostly older men, after an American Legion convention in Philadelphia. Within a year the cause of that disease was determined, and a treatment was discovered. The disease, Legionnaire's, rapidly became a medical footnote. We assumed the same thing would happen with this new disease. We waited. A year later 450 deaths had occurred and thousands were sick, but there was nothing happening—no research, no public health response, no money, and nothing was known except that it occurred primarily among gay men. More months passed, and the only discussion was what to call it—GRID, gay compromise syndrome, gay lymph node syndrome, gay plague, gay cancer, homosexual syndrome—before adopting the more benign Acquired Immune Deficiency Syndrome (AIDS). The year 1982 saw the rise of anxiety, anger, and activism in the affected communities and their allies. The social backlash started to raise its head.

Gay men started grassroots organizations that sought to educate and support people at risk, but there were so many conflicting issues. Gay men were accustomed to being invisible in a society that was fiercely homophobic. For many, being open about their sexuality meant instant ostracization from family, work, and society. Violence, particularly from law enforcement, was common and tacitly accepted. Harvey Milk, an openly-gay elected official, had been assassinated just a few years before. There was the risk of losing the few freedoms that had been won in the preceding years, and there was talk of quarantines, restricted travel, and punitive laws.

Politicians followed the neoconservative dogma of the time and never spoke of the disease in public and, in private, refused to be associated with anything that might be interpreted as supporting gay men. Religious leaders saw AIDS as proof of their bibli-

cal interpretations regarding sexuality and refused to support the spiritual needs of those affected or dying. Public health officials knew how to proceed, but a rabidly-homophobic federal administration silenced them and strangled any funding.

In spite of the resistance gay men and lesbians and their allies persevered. Local AIDS projects sprang up around the country, forming alliances with any organizations that were even remotely sympathetic. Courageous people gathered, raised funds, strategized, lobbied, and protested. Change happened slowly and was mostly on a local level in large urban areas. Outside of progressive urban areas ignorance, ostracizing and risk-taking were the rule. It would be 1985 before a meaningful, coordinated public health response, such as what occurred after the outbreak of Legionnaire's Disease, would begin. According to the Centers for Disease Control and Prevention (CDC), 47,000 people were dead of AIDS by 1987.

On Prison

I was in prison for eight years. I was guilty of what I was convicted of and never denied it. I publicly apologized, paid restitution, and made every effort to make things right. I was fully responsible for what I did, and I carry enormous remorse with me. I cannot change what happened, but I can change the only thing over which I have control: me. Prison was about me.

I can also try to change some of the egregious wrongs that go on behind bars. The current approach to incarceration in Oregon prescribes long sentences in prison for first-time offenses with no attention to mitigating factors (mandatory minimums). Young people are incarcerated with lifetime felons where they learn criminal behavior. Punishment for transgressions while in pris-

on far exceeds the wrongdoing. Inmates can be locked in their cell for days for not wearing a belt. Month-long solitary isolation in "the hole" is handed out frequently and arbitrarily. Nearly half of the people in prison have a mental health diagnosis, but there is little to no psychiatric care. Chemical dependency and drug addiction drive many criminal behaviors, but counseling and support is very limited and follows a one-size-fits-all approach that ignores individual needs. Many inmates lack education either because of lack of access or unmet special needs. Basic high school level education is available in some institutions, but special needs educators are scarce and not universally available. Education beyond high school equivalency is very expensive and requires so many layers of approval that it is only available to a privileged few. Technical skills training would benefit many but in reality is only available to an occasional person who has the skills and support to fight for it. Preparation for release and transition support is minimal and is not tailored to the needs of the individual. Recently released inmates are often back in the same social situation they experienced before prison. Thirty-forty percent are back in prison within a few years and start an endless cycle of recidivism.

The only people who truly know what goes on in prison are those who have been there. The easiest approach to the problems is to move on and forget it after you leave. Since there is minimal oversight of the Department of Corrections, that approach assures that nothing will change. That type of "head in the sand" behavior is what slowed our early fight for gay rights and slowed progress in the early fight against AIDS. I am determined to keep the fight for respectful treatment of people in prison alive. I am willing to be as visible as necessary and spread the word about how the current incarceration system damages more than it helps and provides little incentive to improve.

Did being gay cause difficulties in prison? No. I was openly gay as were many other inmates. No one cared about your sexual orientation. There is far more homophobia in society than I ever experienced inside. If someone didn't like gay men, then they stayed away from us, and as a gay man I avoided them also.

Was life terrible in prison? There were bad things, but you chose how to react to them. Limited activity, closed cell doors, boredom, and relentless proximity to unpleasant people were all things that made for difficult days. If you embraced what you had, it made for an easier time. I did everything that I could. If an activity was available, I took it; if a book appeared on the shelf, I read it; if a new job was posted, I applied for it, and I didn't rue the things that I couldn't do.

What was it like being around all those terrible people? This is the question that I abhor. There are many wonderful people in prison. I would rather spend time with some of them than many people I know on the outside. I continue to write and visit my friends behind bars. They are too often in prison for single errors of judgment that people on the outside have also done. The ones on the inside just got caught.

I was blessed to have a loving support group on the outside that supported me in ways too numerous to enumerate. The support inmates received often correlated with their success in prison and when getting out. Yet, society is all too ready to discard these people. Oregon prisons are referred to as human warehouses, and that is true. Mental health care, personal growth instruction, meaningful activities, and worthwhile jobs are vanishingly rare or nonexistent and only available to people who know how to fight for them.

One friend struggled to find a way to support me while I was in prison, so he sent a postcard with a single word on the back each week. I loved having those cards in my hand knowing that he had held it also. We can provide that kind of support for people in prison and make a difference in their lives. Over 95 percent of those currently incarcerated will be released to the community to be our neighbors. A small token of support can assure that you will have the kind of neighbor you would like to have. It will also break the cycle of incarceration that finds people in and out of a system that has no ability to help them.

Scott (he/him) was born in northwest Portland and now lives there again 70 years later. He spent as much time as possible in eastern Oregon while growing up. Oregon was home for college and graduate school, until a job in Minnesota took Scott on a 20 year journey into AIDS care and research. He was drawn back to the beauty of Oregon and a less stressful job in 1998. Scott has settled into a quiet peaceful existence in the place he loves.

Finding Myself

By Rudd Canaday

I **should have known.** In 1953, when I was 15 years old, all the clues were there. I knew I was attracted to men. In the showers at school, I was afraid I would get an erection, although I never did. I believed, though, that I was not homosexual. (The term "gay" was not used until much later.) Back then most people, including doctors, thought homosexuality was a mental illness. I believed homosexual men wanted to wear dresses and wanted to be women. Sex between men was considered perverted, disgusting, and illegal. "Of course, I wasn't homosexual," I told myself. So I decided most men were attracted to other men. They just never acted on it.

I got married shortly after college. I thought I was in love. Looking back, I believe I got married to hide the fact that I was gay from others and also from myself. For the next 20 years, I continued to believe I was straight. I cared about my wife, Leslie, an intelligent and interesting person, and our two sons. I was reasonably content with my job and my hobbies of woodworking and computers. What I did not have was friends, but I didn't wonder much about that at the time.

Things changed in 1980 when I attended a workshop about sexism sponsored by my employer, Bell Labs. The three-day workshop, *Women in the Work Environment*, was led by a charismatic woman, Elsie Cross. She was assisted by a volunteer from Bell Labs. There were 18 attendees. I enjoyed the experience and was impressed by Elsie. Afterwards, she asked me if I was willing to train to be an assistant. I agreed.

My training took place out of town at the Newark Hilton, where we all stayed for the three-day workshop. Early on the second day, Elsie divided us into three groups of eight participants each. My group had two women and six men. We sat in a circle and, as instructed, each of us pretended to be the person on our left. We talked about ourselves and our lives but always as if we were the person on our left. It was a remarkable experience. As I pretended to be the woman sitting on my left, I really felt that I knew her, almost that I became her. Everyone else in the circle had similar experiences. The person on my right, a stranger, really KNEW me, my hopes, my fears. It was profound, uncanny, disturbing.

When Elsie saw what was happening in our group, she let us continue well beyond our allotted time of 45 minutes. She moved the other groups to the far side of the room so that the training workshop could continue quietly without disturbing us. We continued in our circle for more than two hours until it was time to break for lunch. We were all profoundly shaken by the depth and intensity of the experience.

At lunch, I happened to be sitting at the same table as Elsie. Suddenly, in the middle of lunch, I said, "I have no friends," and I started crying uncontrollably. Elsie and a couple of others took me aside and sat with me, encouraging me to let out my grief. After a while, we rejoined our group and continued the training workshop. I felt exhausted, wrung out, yet very peaceful. That night I slept profoundly well. I felt better than I had in a long time.

Even though I liked my coworkers at Bell Labs, I had always maintained a distance from them. After the workshop, this changed. One time, walking down the hall with a coworker, he remarked about my personal space. He mentioned the separation I maintained between myself and others was much smaller since the training. He was right. I had started letting people in.

My memory of the next couple of years is fragmentary. I remember almost nothing of my work at Bell Labs. I have several very intense memories of individual events in my personal life, but very little sense of how they fit into a chronology. Fortunately, I have a diary that covers the first half of that period, from the 1980 training workshop to

February 1981. Reading my diary now, I realized I was feeling more like a confused teenager than an adult. I was trying to come to grips with my life, my emotions, and my sexuality. At work I probably appeared to be my normal, rational self, but I doubt I was very effective in my job. All of my energy was focused on my inner turmoil.

Roger, a member of my department, told me about a four-day encounter group designed to bring the participants closer together to explore their emotional issues. I liked my boss, and I persuaded him to have Bell Labs fund the opportunity for my department to attend. Participation was voluntary. Thirteen men and two women plus me and my boss gathered at Hudson Guild Farm in Andover, New Jersey, for the encounter group. The experience was profound. I have a photo of me, my fellow attendees, and my boss all in a big "puppy pile" on the lawn.

We all became close and shared intimate details of our lives. Everyone felt that the encounter group had been good for us and good for our department. For months afterward we would all hug one another at work each morning. This was not at all normal behavior for employees of Bell Labs in the '80s or even, probably, today.

After we got back, people from other departments asked me if I recommended doing an encounter group. I said no because I thought it could be too dangerous even though ours had gone so well. In retrospect, an encounter group was a dangerous thing to do because, as a company-sponsored event, employees might feel pressured to participate. In such a setting, people can easily reveal much more than they intend to. It might even precipitate an emotional crisis.

After the encounter group, I started a men's group with eight male employees from my department. I didn't want to lose the closeness we felt in the encounter group. The first meeting was just three months after our training workshop. It became an intense group experience. Like the encounter group, we shared intimate details of our lives. Also like the encounter group, this was both strange and unwise. I am surprised that the other men were willing to be so open and vulnerable with me since I was their boss. But, so far as I know, it worked out well for all of us. At one meeting of the men's group, we talked about the people with whom we felt closest. Most of them said I was the one to whom they felt closest, the one with whom they could talk most freely. I think this is remarkable, again since I was their boss.

Roger, who had suggested the encounter group, was also in the men's group. He wanted us to do nude massage. I really liked this idea, but the others were unwilling, so it never happened. That's probably for the best. I already was blurring the boundaries between what was work and what was personal in a big way.

I started telling a few people that I thought I was bisexual. My wife, Leslie, and I started talking much more than we had in years. I shared with her my need for my own friends, and that I wanted to remain faithful to her.

I developed a close friendship with Bill, a fellow member of the men's group. We would talk and hug for hours. In my diary I wrote, "We held hands for a long time, fondling and exploring each other's hands." For me it felt very sexual, but for him he said it was not. He defined himself as straight, but looking back I don't think he was. I think that, like me, he was torn between his marriage and his gay feelings.

Leslie felt threatened by the men's group and by my friendship with Bill. I was afraid I was losing her. In my diary I wrote, "I want a warm and caring relationship (with a man) but will try to avoid a very close one." Warm, caring, and not close doesn't make any sense, but I was trying to reconcile my conflicted feelings. I knew from the beginning that casual sex would not work for me.

I was still unclear about my feelings—one moment believing I was gay and the next denying it. I think Leslie understood what was going on better than I did. I don't remember when I told her that I was gay; probably much later. But I remember her response vividly. "I've known you were gay since before we were married," she said. And I believe she did know. Her father left when she was 2. The strongest father figure during her childhood was an openly-gay, flamboyant man.

My diary is silent from October 20, 1980, until February 15, 1981, when there is a final entry that really surprises me: "So much has happened and I now realize (believe) that the homosexual issue is a red herring. I am not and never was homosexual. I can feel deep sexual attraction to those I love, male or female." I don't remember where that belief came from. I suppose it was just me not able to admit to myself I was gay.

It wasn't long after my final diary entry in February 1981 that I could no longer deny I was gay. My attraction to men became undeniable. I needed some guidance. Fortunately, a gay couple had a country weekend house about a mile away. I barely knew them, but I decided to approach them anyway. One Saturday I left on my bike, ostensibly to go for a ride, but actually I just rode the mile to their house. I saw the younger man, David, in his yard. I walked up to him and said, "Hi. I'm Rudd. I'm gay, and I don't know anything about the gay world. Can you give me some advice?" He replied that he did not know much about the gay world either because he was in a committed relationship and had little to do with the gay world. But he would tell me what he could.

Over the next couple of months, I went every Saturday on my "bike ride," which actually was an hour or two spent with my new friends, David and his partner. I didn't tell Leslie. Finally, the time came when I no longer could deny I needed to experience gay sex. I'd always been repelled by the idea of anonymous sex, so I needed to find a creative solution to my problem. I decided to approach David.

One Saturday on my weekly visit, David was home alone. I told him of my dilemma and asked if he would be my first gay sexual partner. He was hesitant to do this, both because he saw it as a big responsibility and because he and his husband were supposed to be monogamous. David was in his forties, and his husband was in his seventies. So I wasn't surprised to find out that David had slipped up on his vows a few times. He tried to keep these slips a secret.

David felt it was a bad idea for me to seek my first gay sexual partner in the city. Looking back, it is clear he was attracted to me. He realized that it would be much better for me to have him as my first gay sexual partner, so he agreed. I still thought that perhaps once I experienced gay sex, I would realize that I was not gay, so I decided not to tell Leslie about David. Thus, both David and I needed to find a way to meet in secret. I was scheduled to attend a three-day conference in Princeton, 30 miles away. We decided that I would drive up to his country house from Princeton, and he would drive out to meet me from New York where he lived with his husband. He would find some excuse to be away for the evening but not tell his husband that he was coming to their country house. We set the date and agreed to meet at 6 p.m.

I arrived a bit before 6 and parked in David's driveway to wait for him. Although I was less than a mile from my house, I knew the chance of Leslie driving by and noticing my car was miniscule. Six p.m. arrived, but David did not. As time passed, I became more and more worried. Had David changed his mind at the last minute? Finally, about 7:30, David arrived. He was very upset. In addition to the tension of cheating on his husband, he was unhappy that his being delayed in bad traffic had kept me waiting for so long.

Finally, though, we were together. The setting was quite private. We kissed for the first time, my first real kiss with a man, and then we walked up to the house. The entrance to the house was through a screened porch. Before opening the screen door, David warned me that opening the door to the porch triggered the burglar alarm. So now David had just three minutes to get to the front door, unlock it, go in, and disarm the alarm. I waited outside. David opened the screen door, went to the front door, and tried to unlock it. His key did not work. He struggled frantically to no avail. Apparently, the key, recently cut, was defective. The burglar alarm went off, making a lot of noise.

After a short wait that seemed way too long, with the alarm blaring, the police arrived. David now had to convince the police not to call the emergency number for this address because it was the number for his New York apartment where his husband was. Finally, they agreed that he owned the house so there was no need to call New York.

We still had to get into the house and turn off the alarm. David called their cleaning person who lived nearby. She came over and unlocked the door for us. I don't remember if I hid from her, but of course, David was afraid that she would mention this to his husband. David just hoped she wouldn't.

By the time we got into the house and the cleaning person left, David was a wreck. I, of course, was very nervous, too. I had no idea what to expect from my night with David. Not a recipe for a successful night of sex. We undressed and got into bed together. My first time in bed with anyone but my wife and with a man no less. But once I was there, it felt right.

Since David's house was on a country road, there wasn't much traffic at night. In the two hours or so that we spent in bed together, I don't think more than four or five cars passed by. But every time one came by, David sat bolt upright in bed, afraid it was his husband. Despite all of this, we did make love together, and it was the best sex I had ever had. For the first time in my life, I understood what sex was all about. I knew without a doubt that I was gay; that I had always been gay.

The next week David and I met for lunch in New York. I thanked him for a transformative night. We agreed that, under the circumstances, we should not try for a repeat performance. I believe had we not both been in relationships, we might have fallen in love. I never saw David again. I've always been grateful to him for being my first gay sexual partner, and for being so supportive and loving, and for making my first gay sexual experience so positive despite its drama.

After months of vacillating—I'm bi, I'm gay, I'm bi, no actually I'm straight, I'm gay, I'm bi—I finally knew for certain that I was gay. Leslie and I needed to figure out how to handle it. I was still in love with Leslie, and I was also afraid of being alone. But I also knew that I needed gay sex. I still did not like the idea of anonymous sex, but I did not see any other viable route. Leslie and I decided to open our marriage. I would have one day a week to go out and find gay partners.

This lasted only a few weeks. I went to gay bars in the Village in New York, but I never connected with anyone. I felt guilty, and Leslie felt abandoned. After a few weeks, we realized that an open marriage did not work for either of us.

Leslie was vehemently opposed to divorce. She came from a conservative New England background. You honored your promises no matter the cost. In our marriage vows I had promised "'til death do us part" and, for Leslie, that was the end of the discussion. But I knew I could not stay sexually faithful to Leslie. We decided on a trial separation.

I needed to tell my two sons, ages 17 and 20, that I was leaving Leslie. I was worried about their reactions because, so far as I knew, they didn't know I was gay. As it turned out, they didn't seem surprised that I was gay, but they were quite upset that I was leaving their mother. They both were worried for her. I was confident she would be okay, and in the end it turned out I was right. She had been drinking heavily for several years before we separated, but soon after our separation, she stopped drinking. She went on to make several new friends.

One of my friends offered me an affordable, furnished rental home. Perfect! Leslie asked me to stay home through Christmas. Early in January 1982, as soon as the boys were off to school, I moved my essential stuff to the new house. It took five trips with my small car stuffed to the gills. I remember driving into my new garage on the last trip and feeling a tremendous sense of relief. It was as if a huge weight was suddenly lifted from my shoulders. That was the moment I finally realized that my marriage was really over. I was 43.

Nine years later I met the love of my life. He and I have been together now for 34 years.

Rudd (he/him) is a computer scientist, best known as co-inventor of UNIX. In addition to his Ph.D. in Computer Science, he earned a Master of Divinity degree when he was 52. His religious career was brief, but he met his husband of 33 years when preaching one evening. After leaving the ministry, Rudd founded three software companies and wrote gay romance novels under the pen name Alex Head (amazon.com/author/alexhead). Rudd is now 85 and fully retired. He enjoys classical music, reading, walking daily, Pilates and writing computer programs.

Finding Myself

Missing People

By Rowan Everard

It was the spring of 2018, and the air was thick with fear and suspicion. For several months, a far-right gang called the Proud Boys[1] (later of January 6th fame) had been driving into Portland to harass, threaten, and ultimately assault any queer people they could find. Full cans of beer, then rocks, were thrown at several queer and trans people. A group of partiers coming home from a gay bar were jumped by goons in an unmarked white van. A Black trans woman was found dead in what certainly seemed like a lynching in nearby Vancouver, Washington. Everyone guessed who was responsible. The police, known to be friendly with the Proud Boys, showed very little interest in making arrests.

It was in this climate of justified terror that Tony went missing. I knew him only distantly, as someone who came to events at the Q Center, a local queer community space. He was five or 10 years younger than me, and like me, he was a trans man. Unlike me, he was Black, and when he disappeared, the trans community had a lead-stomach suspicion about what had happened.

Through the likely antifascist channels, organizers spread the word that no one was bragging about the killing or abduction of a young Black trans man. It didn't mean they *hadn't* done it, but it did suggest something approaching innocence. Maybe. On a Thursday in March 2018, the call went out for people in the queer community to look for a missing person. The days were long and tense as the weekend approached. By day I was an acupuncturist, treating queer and trans people with chronic pain. By night I was part of a street medic collective that worked to support protests and marches. The Black Lives Matter Movement was gaining steam in this period. We were asked to attend a rally that Sunday in case the Proud Boys or the police caused trouble. I came partly to support the event and partly to meet a woman I'd been chatting with on a dating app.

She was a spritely blonde vegan who worked at a local college and also did organizing on the side. After finding each other at a modern art statue by the riverfront, we made shy small talk and camped out in the back with the medics to watch the speeches. We stood in quiet respect, scanning the crowd for threats as we flirted carefully in the pauses between speeches. As I began to relax, I felt insistent vibrations from the phone attached to my backpack. With anxiety and a hardening sense of resignation, I checked my messages. A search party had found Tony. Would the medics come to support the situation? I gave apologetic goodbyes to my date. Duty called.

With a sense of considerable dread, my fellow medic, Elsa, and I packed our supplies. Together we left the rally and headed north to Tony's house. Elsa's old blue hatchback rumbled and knocked as we rode in pensive silence. We didn't know what awaited us, but the strong implication was that Tony had been found dead. Should we bring tea? Snacks? Calming herbal tinctures? We decided on all three: chamomile tea, Fig Newmans, and a soothing tincture of skullcap and lemon balm. An herbalist friend of the collective resupplied us continually, recognizing our need for anxiety treatments.

Why hadn't we created a protocol for this kind of situation? There had been a steady drumbeat that marked the deaths of so many trans people over the past few years, coinciding with increased media visibility and reactionary fascist harassment. Many of these deaths were remote from us—a Black trans woman murdered in Atlanta, a Chicana trans woman found dead and probably murdered in LA. Others were closer, like the White trans woman in Portland who had died by suicide in 2017. I hadn't met her, but I had followed her on social media and friends of mine had known her personally. Recently, my friend Adam's lifelong friend, a White trans man, had ended his life after receiving a terminal diagnosis. With each loss, the drumbeats were louder.

It felt like death was coming for all of us. All we could do was bring tea and other medicines, provide some care, and remind people that they weren't alone.

As Elsa and I bumped along I-5 north, past the convention center towards Tony's place, I thought back to the most important queer person I had lost—my first love, Jen.

My memories drifted back to my high school years as I remembered Jen. I was just a 15-year-old kid then. I didn't transition to living as a man until college, so I was moving through high school as a newly-out butch lesbian. I didn't have any experience with girls yet, so when Jen asked me out, I immediately and enthusiastically accepted.

Jen was a glamorous, mysterious senior, and I was just a freshman. She was a skinny, blonde, goth girl—all fishnets and finger armor. She loved Nine Inch Nails, Johnny the Homicidal Maniac, and messing with her conservative grandparents who had raised her when her parents proved to be unreliable. I had willfully ignored a color guard of red flags in falling for her. Three of the most pertinent red flags were her obvious frailty—she always wore an oxygen mask, her complicated relationship with her recent ex-boyfriend, and her closeted status.

No one but her closest friends knew that she was bisexual or that I was her girlfriend. Her long-time friends treated me warily and kept me at a distance, probably as a result of mingled homophobia and maybe something deeper. Jen's right lung collapsed when she was a sophomore in high school—a complication from a near-fatal illness when she was born. The decline in her health was steady after that, and though she was on the organ donor list, her name would not come up soon enough to save her. Loving Jen and preparing for her imminent death bound her friends together tightly. They found it hard to let someone new in, especially someone who seemed as naive as I must have. For my part, I refused to understand how ill she was on any conscious level. While others mourned and prepared, I stubbornly saw only the present moment.

The present could be painful as well, however. After a few months Jen broke up with me, ending our relationship with cryptic words saying that she just wasn't in the right place for a relationship at the time. Even though I sensed our relationship was floundering, I was devastated because I had fallen deeply and unexpectedly in love with her. We took a theater class together, and even after we broke up, she continued to flirt with me. I couldn't handle the complex mix of anger, grief, and longing that coursed through me as we read lines from *A Midsummer Night's Dream* together ("Lord, what fools these mortals be!"). I asked her to give me some space. With more sorrow on her part than I felt was warranted, she granted my request.

It had been two months since we last spoke, the summer break now well under way. I wasn't current on the latest gossip, and when she died, I imagine her friends had drawn straws to see who would tell me. One evening in early

July, Casey, Jen's close friend, broke the news to me over my family's faded, tan, corded wall phone. "Jen died last night. I'm sorry."

I felt shock and disappointment and full-body feelings of sinking and nothingness. I asked what happened. There was a long pause, then Casey said, "The family doesn't want the story to be public." Nonplussed, I robotically thanked Casey and let the phone slip from my hand back onto the wall. My parents and some of their friends were gathered in front of the television for family time. They were stunned to hear the news and unsure of how to help me. They were also not entirely comfortable with queer relationships, and their attempts to be helpful were awkward. I waved them off, needing to get away.

I took a long, wandering walk around the neighborhood with Cora, a friend who lived down the street and who had already graduated high school. She was an older, wiser lesbian, and I looked to her for advice in all things. In this matter she had empathy, but that was all she could offer me. I was still in shock, and I wasn't making a lot of sense as I repeated the same questions over and over: How did it happen? Who knew first? Was there anyone with her?

Cora didn't know, and of course, I didn't expect her to. I wasn't really asking her, I was asking the night sky, the universe, myself. As my shock faded, anger took its place. Why wasn't I good enough to be told the truth? I thanked Cora and we parted ways at her house. Then I sprinted back to my house, animated by the kind of desperation that takes hold of people in moments of crisis. It seemed that if I could just find out how it happened, I could feel closer to Jen. She would still be gone, but I could feel more connected if I only knew the whole story.

I decided to try a different tack with Casey and logged onto my parents' computer, firing up AOL instant messenger[2]. I crossed my fingers that Casey would be logged on, and my luck was in.

Finding her online, however, was where my luck ended. I begged, pleaded, badgered, and used every method of persuasion that I could think of. But as a 15-year-old kid, all I accomplished was making Casey very, very angry with me. So angry, in fact, that she told me that I didn't deserve to know what happened because Jen had never loved me. Jen had loved and cared for many people, but she told Casey what she truly thought of me. The implication of what Casey told me was very bad indeed. Stunned and heartbroken, I typed furiously that I didn't believe her. "Believe what you want," came the quick reply. Casey said that she had called me out of courtesy, and even that was more than I deserved. She said she would see me at the wake in a few days, and I shouldn't get any ideas about learning more then either.

When the time came, I did see Casey at the wake, but only from a distance. Some of Jen's close friends, all 17- or 18-year-old kids, were clustered by the entrance of the funeral home looking gaunt and hollow-eyed. Their parents nearby looked even worse. These were the friends who had given me the cold shoulder when Jen had been alive. Now it was as though I didn't exist at all. I wasn't angry at them. I couldn't fault them for however they acted in this sad moment. Their friend lay semi-preserved in the next room, wearing a baby-blue button-up shirt that she would have detested in life. Jen was done up to look like a perfect angel. They were out of their minds with grief, and I was—what was I? An interloper? A tiny vignette in their larger story? Perhaps I was a ghost, wandering the halls invisibly, mourning in my own private purgatory.

That group of kids were the only people I knew here, and all of them were two to three years older than me. Everyone else was a relative, connected by family bonds I couldn't trace or name. I had met Jen's grandmother a few times since Jen had lived with her, and I saw her in the reception room looking remarkably composed in a sensible gray pantsuit. My parents and I, unsure of what to do exactly, made our way over. Around the room was a cornucopia of flower arrangements, mostly of roses but also star-gazer lilies and carnations. Between these bouquets were poster boards of pictures of Jen from every age. I saw baby Jen, toddler, middle school Jen. Finally, I saw the more recent photographs of Jen as I had briefly known her, wearing black and smiling sardonically.

Here was Jen who had given me my first kiss; the first person to whom I said, "I love you." The finality of her loss started to truly sink in for me then, exactly in the way that a wake is designed to create. I tried to keep the tears in my eyes from falling, and I felt like a stranger in this place surrounded by so many people who had known and loved Jen longer than I had. I didn't want to intrude, nor did I want to give these people power over me.

Jen's grandmother saw my parents and me and made her way over. My father inquired, carefully, about what had happened. The answer—the official family line—was that she had died of a heart attack. With a collapsed lung, her heart was bound to give out at some point, and everyone had braced themselves for the inevitable. I didn't know what I thought about that explanation. It was plausible but also clearly incomplete. Then her grandmother turned to me and said, "And who are you again, dear?"

"I was just a friend," I replied, feeling myself becoming invisible in my sorrow.

The moon hung glassy and pale overhead as Elsa and I approached Tony's house, and I was yanked back from the memories of Jen to the cold reality of the present scene before us.

When Elsa and I arrived at the house, the scene was surreal. For two straight days at that dilapidated old Victorian house, almost everyone had been drinking, smoking pot, and trying to navigate an intense morass of terror, hope, and grief. People coalesced into smaller clumps, some quietly wondering what had happened, others comforting people who were more outwardly distraught. We heard screams coming from the basement and softer voices murmuring in comforting tones to the speaker: "My friend is dead! My friend is gone! What am I going to do?!"

I wanted to go down and help, to let them know that I understood how they felt, but there were so many people in the basement already. Unsure of how to help, Elsa and I set up a tea station in the crimethinc[3]-poster-covered kitchen. We saw the lights of a car pulling into the driveway, then behind the house, and we went out back to find out what was happening.

Elsa and I stepped cautiously into the gravel alleyway behind the house. We joined a throng of people who had just now surrounded the coroner as he arrived, urgent but silent. The oldest person there, a nonbinary trans-masculine person named Fern who was maybe 30, had been talking with all of the officials. The coroner confirmed that Tony's body had been found in a nearby abandoned house, and then he retreated to his anonymous, state-issued van. Turning to us, Fern thanked us for coming, and sighed heavily. We were afraid to ask. Had Tony been murdered? Did the fascists get him? Seeing the question in our eyes, Fern shook their head heavily, between pulls on a cigarette, and nodded toward the coroner's car. "He thinks it was suicide."

Was it relief that I felt then? Tony hadn't been murdered by fascist goons but had chosen to leave this cold world on his own terms. Another dead trans person but at least by choice. At least there was that. I took several deep breaths, working to steel myself against a creeping, subterranean panic and dread.

The alleyway lot was eerily still, and I realized that the person in the basement had stopped screaming. As a small group of Tony's friends approached us, the sound of their shoes crunched softly in the gravel. A trans-masc-looking person of maybe 23 asked if one of us would go with them to the house where Tony had been found to watch the police take the body away. The group was dressed in various punk/goth gear—long baggy pants, spiked belts, dog collars, ripped band shirts—things I had worn myself when I was their age. Even though I was only 30 at the time, the distance suddenly seemed like a yawning chasm. The age gap added to the feeling that I was intruding on this private horror movie. I didn't know anyone here except Elsa. This band of grief-stricken friends looked at us with hungry eyes, perhaps wanting an adult to join them. An anchor. I might not be the perfect person, but I was here. I could at least imagine how they were feeling, so I went with them to watch as the police took Tony's body away. Elsa stayed behind to try and calm people down.

In numb silence, we made our way the two blocks over. Such a small distance after looking far and wide for Tony across the city. It was after midnight and a chill mist hung in the air, muffling the sounds of our footfalls. But the night was clear enough that the wan light of a mostly-full moon lit the scene. The mist reflected the light eerily as we watched two cops make small talk, joking and laughing to each other, as they descended the steps into the basement of a boarded-up house. When they emerged with a stretcher, its contents shrouded in a white sheet, their banter continued, far enough away that we could only hear the tone but not its content. It was just another day for them, another dead body. When the ambulance pulled away without any flashing lights, our little group stood silent for a few minutes. I realized that they were all in a kind of grief-stricken trance, and so eventually I murmured that we should probably head back.

For several days afterwards, I believed I was fine. Tony wasn't my friend. These weren't my direct community members. The unease that I felt welling up inside me, however, suggested otherwise.

I took long walks at night in my neighborhood, which had also been Tony's. I heard through the grapevine that his parents were in town taking care of his final arrangements. He had struggled for a long time with depression and thoughts of suicide. I got a third-hand impression of a family carrying out a plan that they had made and had prayed they would never need. I didn't have children, though I wanted them, and I imagined myself in their shoes. I imagined burying my child's body, recovered from the basement of an abandoned house where he had chosen to end his life. Imagined trying to go back to my everyday life after that. My memories drifted back as I thought about Jen's dad and her grandparents having to return to their empty house with whatever secrets lay there. It was too much to think about for long.

A few days after the events surrounding Tony's death, my roommate, Erin, and I took a walk to the neighborhood park. It was early evening and misty, not quite raining but trying to. My friend seemed worried about me, but I shrugged him off. We were both in a pensive mood, and we wandered around the circle of the park without saying much. I happened to look up at a lamppost and my eyes fell on Tony's face. His missing person poster.

A quick scan revealed more posters nearby. His friends must have put these up in the breathless days between him disappearing and his body being found. My roommate and I looked at each other, and wordlessly we began to collect them. We gathered 10 or 15 from the area all-in-all, feeling certain that Tony's friends wouldn't want to see them and wouldn't have the heart to take them down.

I had recently learned the practice of working with ancestors spiritually, not only ancestors of blood but also of queer lineage, and it felt important to connect Tony to that work. So we took the posters back to our house and put them on our ancestor altar where they stayed awkwardly for several days. We weren't sure what to do with them. It felt disrespectful to just recycle them, but we didn't have a fireplace or a bonfire. And anyway we didn't really know Tony. We were two White trans people, witnesses to the aftermath of the death of a Black trans person. We were filled with complicated guilt. What was it appropriate for us to do, to feel, to think?

Eventually, I prayed. I prayed for my well and bright ancestors to speak with Tony's and to pass down whatever healing they could to him and to his family. I prayed, and then I cried. I cried at the unfairness of everything, at how many people had been hurt and would be hurt again by so many systems of human violence. I cried for myself, too, and eventually for all the queer and trans people that I had lost before and would probably lose in the future if I lived long enough myself.

I let myself understand how much Tony's death had brought up my unresolved feelings about Jen's death. I realized in that moment that we carry our dead with us, and new death brings up the old. I cried for Jen then, for the bitter fact that I would never get to compare notes with her all these decades later over coffee or to look back together at the brief time that we dated in high school. I cried for the closure I never got with Jen, never knowing the full story of her death. I shed more tears for the strange and sacrilegious jealousy that I felt for Tony's friends because they, at least, had closure to cling to. It would be several years before I fully unpacked my complicated grief over Jen's death, but realizing the depths of my sorrow in this moment was an important step in moving toward healing. I cried away my self-pity and angst until I could be present again, here in a time when my empathy and experience were needed.

Then I recycled Tony's missing person posters.

Endnotes

1 A right-wing terrorist group who describe themselves as "western chauvinists." They send fighters to protests, attack their perceived enemies in ambush-style melees, and are affiliated with White Power groups across the county like the 3-Percenters, Oath Keepers, and earth-shaking street preachers.

2 For the younger readers, America Online was the first internet services provider to really hit it big in the US, and their dial-up service came with an instant messaging app (AIM for short) that allowed users to message each other if they were both logged on at the same time.

3 An anarchist publisher that produces books, zines, posters, and pamphlets about leftist issues and causes. It is a common gateway into left politics for younger activists and was especially prominent in the late 2000s.

Rowan (he/him) was born and raised in the suburbs of Chicago, where he first began writing at age fifteen. His fascination with his inner world, and the inner world of others, lead him to become an acupuncturist by day, and writer by night. Both practices focus on healing intergenerational trauma by aiding emotional growth and revealing the historical legacies that shape everyday life. He also loves neon colors, tabletop games, and really terribly bad movies.

Boys don't...

By Esmeralda Xóchitl García

The world moves forward in an indiscriminate direction, and here I am. No rhyme or reason, no purpose driven towards an experience. Just dropped here on some spinning atom of existential distress lost in the vacuous black of eternity. So why should it matter? What weight of witness can be gained from a speck gripping a fable of life on the back of a slightly larger speck? Really, it doesn't matter, I guess. Musing only stands to count the nucleotides that make up the narcissistic poison pushed through the umbilical cord. But that doesn't really make sense now does it? It's out of order. And in a world of shame-induced-rules, to be linear is expected should *you* expect your story to make sense to the casual voyeur. So maybe we should start there? Before I became only one person without heritage, the end of my name chopped off in gangrenous self-preservation. Before the threats on groomer-affiliated accusations of my existence ripped those minimalist versions of safety away from me. Earlier than even the literal paternal stoning of a child, petrified and confused by their place in gravity. Before Chemo sponged my brain and deformed my heart. Before an incestuous embodiment of cruelty made the Milky Way spin above me in pain. For some vain attempt at hearing me in coherence, it's best to start in at least a notable beginning.

The TV sat heaving in the living room, clicking frequencies of RHF framed in wooden cabinetry. Stupid-grainy-shadows of White-American lives in post-grunge-fashion and one-liners forced themselves into the living room. Thick suffocation imprisoned in wood paneling, single panes, an air of violence, this was family time. The devil said, "make him a woman" and my ears, 8 years in consumption, forced atrophy into dynamic aggravation, perked up; they caught light emitted in auditory waves. Movies are an escape at times, but sometimes they only remind us of the exhaustion we feel when life ages too early for a child.

Boys don't feel weak.

I didn't know God. One manipulative controlling father is more than enough when your home is Mickey Moused together by a birthing child and a middle-aged Mexican man.

"Make him a woman." God and her lover granted my wish to an undeserving lecher, and all I get is the outline of knuckles across my cheek. There are rules to being a man. I prayed.

Boys don't feel vulnerable.

With no ethereal instruction manual, I proposed in prayer sin as payment for the haven of femininity; the heaven this motion picture mocked me with. It poked voids into the skin with its tease in dull pallid plot points. But that's against the rules, and rule breakers have shaved heads and clutch the bloody jewelry ripped from their earlobes. The rules were broken, and I learned the four-lettered nature of the word "outfit."

Boys don't whimper.

"*Buenas noches, hasta mañana ~~mijo~~.*" A father's words carry sweet and gentle like wolf's bane perfume, oversaturated in its price. This was a beginning, a birthmarked life at conception between the Devil, Hollywood, and the God who never promised to be gentle.

"I want to grow my hair out." I demanded in childish defiance; a fragile voice standing against a landside of force. Blasphemy is my love language, and the rules gave no mercy to sarcastic defiance; God never grants wishes.

Boys don't keep their clothes clean.

With my cancer now dead, and all its gifts unwrapped but not yet set in long-term memory, it'll be up to me to make my life livable. Of course, time is slow when your 11-year-old body is levied with a new status quo of chronically painful existence; what a wonderful gift of medical intervention; my ingrateful lips didn't fray in bitten ignorance. They might have removed the straw from my heart, but the damage was done. My deformed corporeal prison was still weak from the drip of IVs and surgeries, but my resolve had nothing to lose as I regained stubble upon the summit of my crown. "Long hair is for sissies. No son of mine will be a fucking pussy." His tone as final as a blood test. "Warriors shave their heads so that no one can grab them by their hair. Yank their head back. and SLIT THEIR THROATS! Letting them bleeeed out on the battlefield..." I guess they do send children to war.

Boys don't feel fear.

But I could wait it out. Crossfaded laborers rarely can purchase time to pay attention to their children, especially on the wages afforded to brown skin. My hair would grow, as would all the biological forces of life, an act of God in all their indifference.

The Milky Way is beautiful—at least it was. In pictures it centered everything else in defiance of narcissists and histrionics; their excretions flung to the outer indifference of creation. The sky never seems to drop below the clouds here, though, and the stars we do see seem lonely in their drifting fixations.

Boys don't daydream.

You know great uncles are not always great. They spit out promises of drawing the curtains on the sky before spiking your drink. He promised my witness of a galaxy, but it fell short—like the densest pebble weighted in singularity; there was no intention to tread water in his sinking pre-arrangements. Children can't handle their wine I guess, and throats are not the only things to bleed when a sissy's hair is pulled. The Milky Way spun counterclockwise in the minutes that changed the dates unnoticed to us in our sleep; the biggest insult in the galaxy, but—at least the grass was cool against my face.

Boys don't get nausea.

The Milky Way took its place, a bell ringing in a universe overwhelmed in exhortation; in the absence of deified empathy we take our cues from the survivors. The grass, with its earthy humidity, did its best to keep my head from sinking below the daisies.

"They're putting up their FAGGOT PORN posters all over the FUCKING place." *Tío mío*, my paternal uncle. His anti-abortion pinned hat soaked up the sweat from his hating forehead. Personally I think of universities like island nations. The tide of ignorance like water surrounds them like crops of bigotry seeded around an apple tree; its fruit sweet and crisp above the fallow dirt. "Half-naked fairies hugging and kissing an' shit all over the school walls. MEN KISSING MEN! I tear that shit down when I see it, and they can't stop me." My mind drifted through its 12-year-old software, newly installed with a benevolent virus, while they raised their voices to Oaxaca in toast.

```
C:\\DOS>Run
C:\\>FINDmenkissingmen

    >dir1/dir2/file
     The system cannot find the path specified.
    >echo %error%

C:\Users\EGarcia>dir secret.doc     /s /d
                  >dir secret.doc
                  1 file(s) copied
```

"I don't care what kind of perverted shit they do in their own bedrooms, but they need to keep it there. DON'T put it in my face!" A mother's words weigh more than Giles Corey's[1] stones stacked upon my hope; I won't plead guilty when ignored under the burden. Enlightened in ignorance is the proclamation of the 11th commandment: some sissy-sanctioned promise of love is not for ~~boys~~.

> Boys don't like boys.

In the cold muscles grow tight around scar tissue, with jerks of the random crackling static of burnt-out nerves emotionally driven to stoicism. Wishes are not granted to bad children with bad thoughts. My memory recoiled from the shallow grave of wine spilled apathetically onto the Milky Way. Wishes are not granted to children who are bad. Nothing is given to children having "wanted it" as if defined by domestic shell games; the galaxy started spinning again, the sick of energy in moral paradox.

My home street was married to a bowling alley wound out into an awkward "S." Its crowded and disoriented swivel created a game of pinball with the drunken patrons. Street-parked cars acting as bumpers keeping intoxicated barstool residents from becoming gutter balls.

Boys don't do housework.

We all crush in our environment. Expressive experimentation by unqualified social scientists barely out of diapers; we all used to act first in hopes of understanding it later. But no one ever taught me how to control impulse.... Some things we learn through trial and error. He sat next to me in a treehouse that was set as stable as preteen emotions.

Boys don't hesitate.

We built it with pallets stolen from the foundation of a homeless residence, as the residents were too deep in their poppy-seed blackout to notice our clumsy technique. That was before, though, and now irresponsibly tied to a "Y" in a tree—we sat self-conscious in quiet breathing. "So, have you kissed anyone?" My voice is a poorly arranged musical bar of slurring on quarter notes. His feelings of third degrees dropped a confusing signal of emotional temperature. There is a pause that dodges authenticity like reflecting magnets, repelling before one gives in to vulnerable attraction. "Have you ever thought about sex?"

Boys don't admit they don't know.

He moved six feet away in emotional range as his words fell out like packs from a broken cigarette display. "What?! Why would you ask that?! Wha-What do you think?!" I allowed silence to heal the audacity of our verbal rapport and, as he eased back into his body, I turned in accidental want. When his eyes caught mine, I forgot who I was, and I flipped the magnet over. The moment lasted as long as surprise would in a quiet room and as the adrenaline aged, he remembered who I was.

Boys don't get kissed, they kiss.

His retching was rehearsed in juvenile masculinity, a potent monologue of disgust and repulsion. He threatened to tell everyone, but his awareness of internalized shame, or perhaps my tears, sealed his lips; at least he never opened them for me again. My only rapture was in the occasional regretful glance he'd give me in our mimed and reticent conversations; a collision of clandestine semaphores with no cipher.

"Are you straight?" Questions are things that we allow only in knowing the comfort of privacy in our neurological vaults. Non-verbal answers are easy to forget. They exist like extraneous ripples, cold and sprinting across pond water. "You can tell me," she whispered; her hair fell like water providing a curtain between our faces and the outside world as my back provided the foundation of our structure. "I am with you, aren't I?" Questions are answers if you read them in context. Their planted nature is indirect in its growth, and in such irregular patterns one can read the negative spaces in their inflection. "That means nothing." She smiled. A faint displacement in symmetry draws the irresistible bliss that is understanding. The space between middle school and high school is cavernous but enchanting; this is where myths attain their place in Edith Hamilton's[2] pantheon of fallen deities. A script of desires in the sharp lettering of a jammed typewriter, gripping the paper for purpose; she kissed without considering gender. The world spins when the eyes are closed, no expression of faux wet hands under the snap of hospital gloves; my skin felt apart from me, but my heart can feel warmth, even through insulated biology.

Boys don't fall in love.

There is no reintegration though, and the moon, while bright and distracting, cannot take away the backdrop of a spinning galaxy; love is a feeling, not a cure. There is no detour exorcism for emotional lacerations apart from resolving to win a game of chicken, dead or alive. Scars can stop the bleeding, their smooth inflexible sutures felt with every movement from the inside out, but a child is not prepared to confront the radiator of a bus. She held my hand while I crossed the street. Sometimes you can't get home, but 14 feet makes a difference.

In high school the boys are much sweeter. Smearing a queer is a thing, of course, especially that when diagnosed, the cure for a twink is a broken rib. But they can be sweet too. "I'm not a FAG, so don't say shit, okay?" He looked into the green pools used to drown my vision, the hands of my soul stuck to the flank of a horse on the bank; his words here soothed as they burned. In synchronicity his fingers intertwined with my long black curls, betraying the anger in his voice as he threaded his digits through the hair at the nape of my neck.

Boys don't relinquish the lead.

Nighttime adventures end in comfortably chilly and encouragingly unintentional juxtapositions. In the bowl of a skate park, intentions secure us in the moment. I allowed my eyes to blur in suicidal surrender as I curled up with my mind sinking into his fluffy torso. My skin weighted in its anxiety sinks below my soul as the wisps of THC swirl towards the sky like silky ghosts escaping their condensed prisons. "Don't be a fag," he coughed in blush when my hand came to rest upon his soft belly. Boys were sweeter in high school, but boys are still boys even in the millennium.

Boys don't like love stories.

Closeted romance leaves you cold in the winter, and school administrators don't appreciate the funny comfort of crossdressing. A joke is a joke after all, until it feels right. Summer bonfires are cold when he won't touch you, when you are a secret, or when he gets drunk and leaves you on your own in the forest for the sake of indifference. "No Mexicans are allowed to drive my car!" He slurred through the stuttering of tires desperately clinging at the gravel road losing its grip on reality. So drunken and annoyed in his impatience; that's a funny way of saying goodbye.

Boys don't beg.

But little ~~boys~~ can't breathe and cry, not when they are growing as men. He'd be too afraid to tell on you anyway. Walking in the dark, you can convince yourself of anything. It's easier when you are smaller than they are, green is a color that bleeds clear in the dark; even in hetero-drag, they'll ignore you when you cry.

"~~He's~~ drunk! L____[3] can't handle ~~his~~ booze! What a fucking FAG." Boys are not safe people. But it's so easy to ignore the crushing weight of the Milky Way and the exhausting white-knuckled grip of being an indentured thespian when drowning in fermented potatoes.

Boys don't let girls overpower them.

"Is ~~he~~ out? See if you can get his clothes off," she said in intoxicated vernacular. Girls don't always make things safer. The stars cannot always be witnesses to the introductory stickers stapled to our foreheads, "Hello, my name is *Victim*." But they can still be felt; their light burning through the loss of sensation when one has no layers left to protect. "Oh yeah, I don't remember last night..." I gripped my Oscar in A-list skill to control my tone and cadence.

Boys don't get...

Being smaller and weaker is tradecraft when you are Ana's devotee[4]. At the doctor's ~~boys~~ don't have girl disorders; they are to become ~~men~~. Nor are they, in the damp parking lot of some confused pavement puddles, to use their mouth for currency. "Keep the change."

My chin is split like dented clay, a speed-limit sign that invites unconsented touch under disco balls, strobes of flavored light, and the musty dark that corners blown speakers. It's funny the way boys can grow up and still play cops and robbers. Their finger-guns holstered in foreign belt-loops; someone sure shot the sheriff, and it smeared his makeup. He reached from the bar, and I grabbed his hand at the wrist. "I don't play with unwashed hands." My devotion, my pro-motion of Ana took all but a buck thirty from my flesh, but I still had claws.

Boys don't play softly.

His eyes may have caught the game, but a cat will still kick you if you touch her wrong. "Come home with me?" They always say it so overconfident in tone, so annoyed when your iris tags your forehead. His hands looked weak, though, and I don't bruise easily. A decision to leave makes light of the space between atoms and intimacy. By physics we may never touch, but when you are small and sweet you HAVE to build a tolerance to unwanted hands; probing fingers like stinging nettles taking liberty in proximal accidents accidentally on purpose. The door, while swung open, provides no affordable price when encroached on by blind racist bears in predatory intoxication; their ground up profiles read *No Blacks, No Asians, No Latinos*, preferences perdidos when choosers become beggars.

Boys don't run away.

"Lead the way." I looked up, allowing my pupils to open like steel-blued roulette wheels as I shrugged the cylinder into the gap. A Honda is not a home, but sometimes the cold pulls the lid off the sky, and it opens just enough to yank your eyes upward in antithesis of gravity.

Boys don't feel vulnerable.

The Milky Way started spinning again, like flashing yellow lights all disorientated and sobering. Before his key turned the lock, my foot planted in anonymous exhaustion on the turntabled linoleum of the Max.

Boys don't like to play it safe.

I arrived in the reception of a knock. Her door closed behind me, a secure barrier between me and the galaxy's awkward proximity; that familiar gait of sweat and body hair. *"Ay, Chavito, tienes frio?"* Clean hands *y fuerza de nacimiento de alacran;* claws retract into beans under the influence of non-toxic venom. Friends in casual love shred memories to wedge between their feathers like little tropical birds clambering across a coffee table. There is warmth and safety in bilingual assurances, here my skin did not retract, and I slept through an entire dream.

Boys don't want to be held.

Memories seem so distant and tucked away when skin cells introduce themselves like never-separated-puzzle-pieces in tandem of accorded embraces; an exhale can be home until the sky stops spinning.

Curls stick like Velcro to curls, even with my hair removed in professional courtesy, the curls still reach out. My memory resides in the hair that twists around our intentions, and this was the first time it hooked me into consciousness.

Boys don't get swept off their feet.

There have always been rules everywhere, and a college library stacking up its paper-thin arguments makes no room for *malcriadez*. But there they were. Walking through all the inhibitors like a stag through spider webs, only adding to their spired crown like dewy jewels in the spaces between me and my vision. Their curls gripped mine, and I was willing to leave that mire that filled my shoes and anchored my feet. "I'll go with you if you want me to." Their eyes in deep earthy tones defined themselves in monochromatic move-ment; the more curls you have, the more curls that grip.

Boys don't subordinate to ~~women~~.

Warmth and love make time pass unnoticed, but eventually we all catch the sight of sand flowing through glass aper-tures.

"I don't see you anymore." They offered up in an-chored question. In 35 trips around the Sun, delirium has etched its way through my fingers as the ride purposefully ejected my awareness.

Boys don't sit on the pity pot.

Then, at some swollen point my cochlea gave it up, and I spewed my pain into the gravitational well that had bent around me. There is something about wallowing that numbs and erodes in comforting waves. "Who are you?" Their voice dropping accusations into the fading fabric of the one shirt I'd always worn.

Boys don't fuss about clothes.

Men are announced in the domination of brass over the melody of wood. In anger and broken fingernails, I just can't chip away the archetypes set by daytime talk shows.

Boys don't watch Jerry Springer.

If you are not you, they eventually will leave, they always leave, but curls grip tightly into their stubborn nests. "Where is the smile of the man I married?!?" Sometimes walls can harden like scar tissue growing thicker with recurrent cuts.

Boys don't wince in pain.

Sometimes there is a window that sits just to my left, right out of range of my understanding. The walls, too thick to see where it ends, roll out like an angled and crooked tunnel hinting at light ambiguously beyond my spectrum of vision. "Tell me, I'm here!" I can't see through the window, it's too small, and I've long ago painted over its frozen hinges.

Boys don't like pretty things.

~~She~~ stopped asking and the light dimmed in a clouded eclipse. Their fingers gripping the stupid shape of a doorknob, as its polished façade came clambering through my window in creaking clicks, like snagged razor blades gripping dermal cells.

Boys don't react emotionally.

I sink as muscles slack, competing to give up their calcified protection and the curls tug back their attention under the threat of split ends and solitary strands. "I am not your ~~husband~~; I am not L____." Moments unfurl the spacing between sound and time like an unperceived echo, picking at us in the emptiness that silence offers to us in provocation. They peered in as I pushed my fingers through the scar tissue laid tight to my chest, a redlined and discolored monolith toppled onto a child's body. I pull out a shape as my eyes give in, sinking into the arm's reach of my juvenile wish. Whether death or birth, I give it up along with what's left of the air in the room. They hold the shape up to the light and L____'s body lay split on the floor like some fleshy chrysalis. An Emerald Flower, its pedals cracked and frail, but in the light they catch a glimpse of the smile that they remembered.

Boys don't exist as repeating decimals. Not all boys are boys.

Endnotes

1 A character in the play *The Crucible* by Arthur Miller who existed in real life and was executed during the Salem Witch Trials. Giles was killed over the course of multiple days for suspected witchcraft, of which he refused to plead guilty or innocent. The torture technique that was used was called pressing, a process in which stones were continuously stacked upon his chest in attempt to get him to give a plea. Not only did Giles not plea, whenever he was visited by the authorities, he asked them to add more weight.

2 Edith Hamilton is an author who wrote many books on classical mythology. This author became known to many in my specific queersphere as we all seemed to have a pre-

ternatural attraction to her works, and classical mythology in general. While it's argued whether or not Edith was gay or straight, some things go without words, given Edith had a female "companion" and "bestie" that lived with her until death and was even buried alongside her. They were the best of friends.

3 This is in reference to my deadname and used to signify its use in a given situation. Imagine it as a bleeped four-letter word. The same technique is used when referring to some pronouns in the story.

4 This is a reference to the Pro-Ana subculture movement of the 90s and the early 2000s. Pro-Ana was a reference to people struggling with anorexia who viewed it not as an illness but instead as an accomplishment of self-control. The advent of online social media is noted as spreading and promoting this struggle.

Author's Note

The writing style that I used for this story is often a source of questions whenever anyone reads something that I have written. It's complicated, but it does have a purpose beyond that of aesthetics. Before giving my genesis of voice in my writing, however, I want to, of course, give credit to an old idol of mine, Sylvia Plath, a true kindred spirit to a lost, scared, queer teenager who thought that no one would ever understand her. I incorporate a piece of her essence in much of my writing. Specifically, when I wish to invoke her in my process you might spot the phrase "Vac-

uous Black." This one-two punch of pure literary beauty is from my favorite poem of hers, Years, and especially when I am proud of a piece, I incorporate the word "combo" somewhere in the flow as a tribute to her and all she's done for me over the course of my life. But this style for me started when I was young, likely late middle school or early high school. In my world, which was not particularly safe for queer expression, it would not have been safe for me to actually write in a journal; I mean, leaving direct evidence is just asking for someone to read it. So, after reading some Sylvia Plath, wallowing in my teenage dramatic melancholy, I started experimenting with words. I didn't set out to do this as a way to journal incognito, but when I began to see how I could bring myself into a moment and describe it using abstract metaphor, I began to use it to journal. It was like a secret code, of which I will say that, in this story, I have gone to great lengths to make it clear so as to make it more available to my readers. However, in its purest form, it gives me the ability to go back and know exactly what I was feeling at the time of writing it while keeping my experience safe from prying eyes. After reading this, I want to advise you to not worry if you didn't understand or get a reference, its unimportant to the story, and really my story as a whole is unimportant in the grand scheme of things. Instead I encourage you to simply allow your mind to wander through it. That's what I did. This form of writing for me is a window into my internal monologue, my brain like a game of word association. Its modality anchoring the memory to a foundation made of references so that I can not only remember what took place but have a keen emotional echo pieced together by references that have evoked a similar feeling.

Esmeralda (she/her/ella) is an adolescent addictions counselor, leading a team of counselors providing free behavioral health counseling in high schools. She's also a college professor of addiction and multicultural counseling. She is a native of Portland, Oregon, but has lived in other places over the years. She is a biracial Latina and a trans, queer woman. As such, she has molded her chillona voice into that of the behavioral health chingona that makes her voice, and those of her patients, heard across the Pacific Northwest.

Boys don't

257

Our Bold Voices

ourboldvoices
www.our**bold**voices.com

We encourage you to stay connected by visiting us at
www.ourboldvoices.com to follow our current projects.

Made in United States
Troutdale, OR
05/19/2024

19904939R00155